Gifted Workers
Hitting the target

Gifted Workers
Hitting the target

Noks Nauta
Sieuwke Ronner

BigBusinessPublishers

© Copyright BigBusinessPublishers 2016

Translation: Benno Groeneveld & Kathleen Wilson

Illustrations: Ingrid Joustra

ISBN 9789491757297

www.bbpublishers.nl/gifted-workers

Content

Preface

I know perfectly well how you are ... You irritate me no end and you are extremely difficult to deal with. Your extreme intelligence casts a dark cloud over your good characteristics – so nobody can benefit from them ... you criticize everything and everyone, except yourself ... so it is not surprising that you become alienated from the people close to you. Nobody enjoys being corrected or exposed - and most certainly not by such an insignificant little man as you. Who on earth do you think you are? There is no person on earth who can tolerate being criticized by someone with as many personal weaknesses as you have. I think in particular about the disparaging manner in which you use mystical terms to proclaim that something is like this or like that - without considering for one moment that you may be wrong.
If you were not such an annoying little man, you would have been nothing but laughable. But now it is impossible to live with you...
(Fragment of a letter written by Johanna Schopenhauer to her son Arthur.)
From: Yalom, 2005.

Living with a person with a very high intelligence is not always easy, or pleasant, for those around them, as is clearly shown by this quote from a letter to her son written by the mother of the famous - and certainly gifted - philosopher Arthur Schopenhauer, who was 19 years old at the time. We could almost forget that high intelligence is primarily an indication of potential talent. Even of great talent. The more that talent is seen and recognized the better it can work in society and the easier that talent finds a place to fit in.
It is estimated that their talents are only recognized and appreciated in one third of all gifted people. These are the gifted people that perform very well.

But in the case of the other two thirds, their talents are not sufficiently recognized or are not recognized at all. As a result, gifted people may lose direction. This could lead to dysfunctions in their work or private life. In this book, we provide eleven examples of gifted adults who try to find their own way after having lost their direction. Often a trigger from the environment was needed to start their individual voyages of discovery. In a number of these cases this search results in their becoming more balanced and consequently better able to function in society.

What exactly does it mean to be gifted? Highly intelligent people score in the upper 2% of recognized intelligence tests. The numbers may be different for different tests but in general they are higher than 130 or 135. People are supposedly born with high intelligence as a kind of 'equipment' and there is also a physiological and neurological base for this condition.

Some people only classify someone as being gifted if he or she also achieves success in society. This may be true. But who determines what is to be considered a succes in a given case?

Recognizing that a high IQ alone is insufficient to characterize people as gifted, a group of experts (people who are themselves gifted *and* work with the gifted) in the Netherlands conducted a research project in 2006/2007 to determine what the term 'gifted' means. This research led to a theoretical model that resulted in the following definition based on commonly shared characteristics:

A gifted individual is a quick and clever thinker, who is able to deal with complex matters. He or she is autonomous, curious and passionate. A sensitive and emotionally rich person, living intensely. He or she enjoys being creative.
(Kooijman-van Thiel, et al, 2008)

The above-mentioned research, based on the Delphi method, paid much attention to the characteristics of the gifted with the following being the most notable:

- highly intelligent (thinking)
- autonomous (being)
- many-facetted emotional life (feeling)
- passionate and curious (wanting)
- highly sensitive (perceiving)
- creation-directed (doing)
- sparkling, original, quick, intense and complex (interplay)

Based on this model we recognize that characteristics themselves can be seen as neutral, but in real life they can lead to pitfalls and barriers. Being extremely sensitive may lead to problems if one is exposed to too many stimuli. Being very autonomous may lead to problems with cooperation. Being a highly intelligent thinker may lead to becoming very narrow-minded and not open to discuss emotions and connecting with others.

In principle, this 'equipment' allows one to have intense experiences and accomplish fantastic achievements. Each gifted person has to discover in his or her own way how this can best be done in their own individual case. This often involves trial and error. There are no general rules.

Being gifted obviously is not a disease or an abnormality. However, from a statistical point of view, the characteristic 'extremely high intelligence' could be considered as an extreme deviation from the norm. Many gifted people also experience feeling different from others, starting with their earliest memories. 'What is wrong with me?' or 'What is the matter with me?' they often think.

In a way similar to how extremely tall people must be alert to their environment as they would otherwise frequently bump their heads, gifted people may also find it useful to be very alert to possible threats from their environment.

In the same way very tall people can choose careers in which their height could be an advantage, gifted people may also make choices that suit their talents. Finally: tall people sometimes require special surroundings, e.g. with furniture. The same applies to gifted people in both their home and work environments.

Very little research has been done around gifted adults. In this book we have combined our own experiences in working with gifted people with the general expert knowledge that we obtained as occupational physician, Work and Organizational psychologists, and also as coaches. We do this by providing examples, lifted from our actual work, of gifted employees who ended up in one of the gifted person's own traps and losing direction as a result. To help us deepen our analysis, we have set up a long-term multidisciplinary peer expert group with professional counselors of gifted people. At the time of writing nothing else like this existed.

The sequence of the chapters is not arbitrary. The examples provided in chapters 8 through 11 deal with people who are not only gifted but may also have a mental disorder, a personality disorder (chapters 8 and 9), an autism spectrum disorder (chapter 10) and ADHD (chapter 11). Whether these special characteristics occur relatively more frequently in gifted people is still a source of speculation.

In each example we start with analyzing the present situation. We discuss the subject's actual behavior and the way the people around him or her respond. We look at the cognitive facts (the intellectual reasoning), the emotions and the motivations of gifted people. We indicate when and how the expertise of professionals might be used to stimulate people who find themselves in such a situation.

At the end of each example, we recap, outlining our own perspective regarding the case, and we provide several practical tips. At the end of the book we provide a summary chapter, which outlines some themes that seem to frequently come up among gifted people. These serve as a kind of review of all the cases described. In order not to lessen the readability of the book, specific professional terms and methodologies are explained in a separate chapter. Finally, we provide a list of literature and websites that were used or consulted for this book.

These examples, we hope, will make it easier to recognize problems faced by gifted people in their jobs, both by the gifted themselves and by those in leadership positions, occupational physicians, psychologists or career coaches. Employers, human resource employees and others who come into contact with gifted employees, also can benefit from this book.

The goal is to help recognize talent, even when it is hidden, acknowledge people's gifts and help the gifted and their talents grow and flourish.

Caveat on the personal stories described
Particularly in the case of gifted people - who tend to have fairly colorful interests and a unique career - a true account could very easily result in the person involved being recognized or traced through the Internet. We therefore created the examples provided in this book from the elements of stories of different people, while retaining most of the color and the themes of their lives. This way, we hope to protect the privacy of our clients, their friends and acquaintances.

Acknowledgements
During the translation Andrew Aus from the UK proof read and corrected our language for proper English phrasing and terminology. Jakub Oblizajek from Poland helped us in finding relevant information on High IQ societies. Karel Jurgens helped us with a lot of editing, and more.

1. I think my manager is stupid!

For several months, Liz Snyder has been a trainer/advisor at a national training institute. She is 45 years old and has considerable experience in developing training programs and providing training courses. Her colleagues find her to be cheerful and self-confident and she knows how to support them. She communicates in a very direct way. Some of her colleagues like this, but others find it hard to take. Liz has a good relationship with her closest colleague, not only because of the quality of her work, but also because of her enthusiasm and sense of humor.

Her manager is one of the people who can appreciate her mild provocations. Liz finds him to be a pleasant, easygoing man, who is open and interested in her experience. Together with another colleague, she meets with her manager regularly to discuss new developments in the organization. For instance, her manager would like to start a new type of service for the company's clients. Liz has many new ideas and she notices that he actually uses many of them. Liz feels appreciated and enjoys her work. Her clients are also happy with her work.

Two months after she started her job, her manager leaves and is replaced by an interim-manager, Kurt Spindler. Suddenly, Liz is no longer involved in anything. So she decides to take the initiative and makes an appointment with the new manager. During her first conversation with Kurt, she notices a number of things. Kurt appears to have poor body hygiene. He has a strong Northern accent. She also sees that he keeps his racing bicycle in his office. Liz is struck by the fact that Kurt seems to know little about the organization, and he has no clue what Liz is doing. As a result she has little confidence in what he is doing. Liz has very clear ideas about how to improve the service provided to the clients and innovative ideas about product development. But Kurt shows no interest at all in her ideas. Instead, he considers her stubborn and critical.

For the next two months, she sees no change in Kurt. On the contrary, Liz has the impression that he is more often off on his racing bike than working. She notices that Kurt increasingly goes out of his way to avoid her. In meetings he does everything he can to shoot down her comments. Liz feels that she is not being heard or appreciated.

For months nothing happens in the organization. No new products are developed and Liz hears nothing more about improving services to clients. The income of the organization declines and Liz becomes increasingly concerned. Liz discusses this with her colleagues and explains her ideas. A number of them share her concerns and one of them proposes that Liz should become part of a think tank set up to provide ideas to the interim-manager. Liz is eager to do so, but faces fierce opposition from the new manager, who makes it clear that she will only become part of the think tank 'over his dead body'. This really infuriates Liz. But, because of her strong commitment to the organization, she does not give up.

In the meantime, the colleague with whom she worked most closely has left and no replacement was appointed, so Liz has lost her sparring partner. She takes her responsibility towards the clients seriously. She works fast and takes on the work of her missing colleague. This means that she has to work much harder and longer, while at the same time feeling less and less appreciated. Liz becomes short-tempered and is increasingly irritated by the mistakes of the secretaries and, obviously, also by Kurt's stupidity.

Management demands that Kurt take action, directing him to prepare a proposal for a full reorganization. Kurt asks a few of his advisers to read his plan and Liz also sees the document. When Liz asks critical questions, Kurt realizes that his proposal is fairly weak, but tries not to reveal his own concerns. However, Liz notices this immediately. Eventually, Liz offers to rewrite the proposal and to incorporate her own ideas and the ideas of her colleagues in Kurt's proposals. Her colleagues support her ideas, and she rewrites the proposal within a very short time.

Her colleagues praise Liz's plan, but Kurt does not respond. When Liz sees the draft submitted to management a few weeks later, she sees that the document consists largely of her own text, but Kurt is listed as the sole author. Liz explodes. She feels she has been taken advantage of and that Kurt is both terribly stupid and underhanded.

The relationship between Liz and Kurt deteriorates even further. When Kurt fails to do anything to recruit a new adviser to replace Liz's colleague who left, Liz can take it no longer. She calls in sick, because she suffers from hyperventilation and stomach complaints.

Analysis of the situation
Liz strikes you as a lively and self-confident employee who feels a strong commitment to her work and her clients. She has a good understanding of her clients' needs and is able to develop and implement creative training programs. She communicates well with her closest colleagues and feels appreciated by her original manager. He provides her with many opportunities, which means she is able to use her talents to the full.

Things go wrong when a new manager is appointed. This man probably feels threatened by her critical attitude from the beginning. Liz displays all the characteristics of a gifted employee (astute and insightful, perfectionist, high standards, creative), with all of the problems that result from it. Yet, she seems unaware of this.

Reflection on the situation

Liz makes an appointment with her occupational physician.[1]
noot Together they look at her situation.

Liz is extremely stressed and negative about her work situation
and her own performance. She responds emotionally, feels
guilty and blames herself for staying in this job much too long.
Her occupational physician tells her that she has many
symptoms of being overworked.
Liz feels that her work is a constant source of tension and
has developed a number of physical and psychological
problems. It appears that her work load and her ability to
take responsibility have been unbalanced for quite some
time. For this reason, the occupational physician advises
her to take two weeks off on sick leave to gain some perspective on her work situation.
Liz completely disagrees, believing that the conflict with
her manager needs resolution. She contacts the company's
employment and organizational expert, who is also a
psychologist.

Learning to deal with obstructive thoughts

In several interviews, Liz tells her story to the Work and Organizational psychologist.[2] Comments from her are summarized
below from the expert's perspective.

I am struck by the fact that Liz mainly blames herself and
feels that she failed. She feels she should have done things
better. She knows that her manager felt threatened by her

---

1   In The Netherlands occupational physicians are medical doctors, specialized in the
    relationship between work and health. They give advice to employers and employees
    relating to the prevention of work-related diseases and participation (can employees
    with a disease perform their jobs safely?).

2   In the Netherlands a Work and Organizational psychologist is a specialized psycholo-
    gist who contributes to an organization's success by improving the performance and
    well-being of its employees. He or she works either in a company, or in a department
    of Health and Safety, or sometimes is self-employed. These psychologists help people
    individually and operate in the workplace or hold workshops for dealing with work-
    related stress.

and (as she sees it) could not deal with that. She blames herself for this. Liz thinks, irrationally, that she should have done everything perfectly, that she should have made sure that her manager was convinced her proposals were correct, that she should have been able to do her own work plus that of her colleague and in addition take care of her family at home.

It takes quite a while for Liz to develop more realistic expectations of herself. Liz almost drowns in her own emotions and feelings and finds it impossible to look objectively at what went wrong, including the extent to which her manager was responsible. Two weeks of rest to create some more distance – as advised by her occupational physician – seems like good advice.

Yet, Liz finds it difficult to accept this advice because she is scared that she would then completely lose her grip and become even more depressed. We decide to see whether she can do a few small assignments every day, whilst also taking time to rest. I propose that she speaks to a few people who have found themselves in similar situations. Other people who – like her – became overstressed because of their work.[3] After some hesitation, she agrees and actually finds it helpful to share her experiences. She gains insight into her irrational thoughts ('I need to be perfect and successful in every way to be worthy of respect and be appreciated by society. I therefore should not make any mistakes - either at home or at work').

After two months, she is able to see that her manager failed in some things, including in his attitude towards Liz and by failing to appoint a replacement for her colleague. She is also able to see that her insights and solutions for the situation were probably very good but that her manager was not yet ready for them. She understands that she was unable to connect with what her manager was doing.

---

3   There is a more detailed explanation about stress and being overstressed in the information chapter at the end of the book.

We discuss her self-image and her conviction that she should be taking care of *everything*, become like Mother Mary and looking after everyone. She tells me that, when she was young, she had to look after her disabled younger brother. Without her being aware of it, the example set by her perfectionist mother adversely affected her. Liz regains control over her situation when she looks at it more rationally and begins to see that her response is rooted in her past.

Dealing with emotions
Liz is almost literally overwhelmed by her feelings of power-lessness, guilt and anger towards herself and her manager. Liz feels guilt towards her clients and is furious with Kurt, who also did not get in touch with her after she called in sick. She also feels that she failed. If only she had done things differently. Should she not have known that things would end up this way?

Liz has to learn how to put her emotions into perspective. She needs a great deal of time to accept that she has become overstressed as a result of her work and perhaps also because of her manager. Rationally, she now under-stands this well, but emotionally she still experiences feel-ings of failure and guilt.

As a result, Liz becomes very sad and even somewhat depressed, feeling overwhelmed as negative experiences from her past emerge. When she was a child, much was expected of her and making mistakes was not acceptable. She tells me that her mother punished her severely if she did not do the tasks given to her in the way that her mother wanted her to do them. At school, only the highest possible marks were good enough to earn her mother's praise. She suffers much pain from the past, which we deal with by using the ABC model of the RET.

The ABC model and RET

Rational Emotive Therapy (RET) is based upon the theory that a connection exists between feeling, behavior and thought. According to Albert Ellis, the father of RET, these three elements also continuously influence clients' personal goals. These personal goals create different situations (A), thoughts (B) and feelings and behavior (C).

The ABC model uses three steps to define the problem (A), the feelings caused by the situation (C) and what clients think about it (B). By influencing thoughts (B), which, in problem situations, are often irrational and involve negative feelings about the clients themselves and about others, the feelings and behaviors are then transformed to new, healthier ones (C).

From: Ellis & Baldon (2004)

Our interviews show that Liz finds it difficult to feel her emotions. And she does not allow herself to have any positive opinions about herself. Liz has a negative self-image. When I tell her that she may very well be gifted, she is astonished and strongly denies this. But she does tell me that she once achieved a high score on an IQ-test. She says she will read more about it.

We discuss the fact that she is not able to feel emotions, particularly positive emotions. We decide that Liz will receive a form of creative therapy during which she will create paintings of her emotions. Eventually she shows me a few of her paintings. They are penetrating, expressive and colorful. I think they are beautiful. Of course, Liz says that she cannot paint at all. When I joke about this and point out the analogy with her work situation, she finds that hard to deal with, but she is now at least able to laugh about it. This demonstrates that she gained some insight into her negative feelings of guilt and shame about her work.

I ask Liz to write a report about the last meeting she had with her manager and colleagues in an attempt to clarify who did what. She writes a beautiful story, full of detail and humor. Liz has developed a much more balanced perspective about her work situation. She sees that it would be almost impossible for her to change the organization by herself ('It was like flogging a dead horse', she says). We discuss the areas in which she did succeed, something Liz still finds difficult to do. Over time, she gains more insight into the extremely high burden she places upon herself (and others).

Much of her perfectionism can be traced back to the fact that Liz finds it difficult to distinguish between who she is and what she does. In the past, she was mainly assessed based on what she did not do well. As a result, Liz has concluded that she is never good enough.

Based on her new discoveries and an interview about her talents (read: giftedness), we discuss a plan for her returning to work. I ask her about the things that motivate her in her job.

I am struck by the fact that Liz has great difficulty explaining what motivates her. Is this a consequence of her being overstressed, resulting in a lack of energy? I mainly hear her talk about things – all related to the organization of her work – that drain her energy. Although she receives administrative support, she does much of her work herself. In this respect too, Liz demands high quality and doesn't accept mistakes. Mistakes do occur, however, so she prefers to do everything herself. I describe her negative attitude to her, and ask whether she is truly energized by high-quality work, which meets clients' expectations. She seems to be particularly inspired by finding new solutions for clients because this allows her to use her creativity. And she does this very well.

Liz explains that in her current job she mainly misses a sparring partner and buddy with whom she can develop new ideas. Since the departure of her colleague, she is lonely and no longer feels that she fits into the culture of the organization. Yet she seems to enjoy her work. Her resume also clearly shows that what Liz enjoys most is developing and devising new (training) plans and providing advice about organizational development. At this stage, Liz decides that she wants to continue working for her employer. She is still thinking about the kind of work she would like to do later.

How to proceed?

As a result of the interviews with the Work and Organizational psychologist Liz manages to let go of some of her irrational convictions ('I need to be perfect') and her feelings of guilt and shame. She chooses to do the following.

Interview with the personnel adviser
Liz wants to stay at her current job because she finds the work interesting. In order to make it possible to stay she understands that she needs the support of someone within the organization, because she decided not to talk to Kurt. She has gained a more realistic insight into herself, but is still inclined to demand much from her environment. She will discuss this with the personnel adviser. She draws up a list of conditions under which she would be prepared to return to work. How can she express her creativity? What should her attitude be towards her manager and her colleagues? What is the potential of others and what are the limitations of the organization? Liz succeeds in gaining the support of the personnel adviser. He offers her much support, but asks her to consult with her colleagues to find out how she can gradually take on her responsibilities again.

Collaborating with colleagues
Liz has become more aware of her talents. She finds it easier to be flexible, is very emphatic, thinks quickly, is able to empathize with her clients and is creative when developing

new training programs. Instead of expecting others to work the same way, she offers to create made-to-measure programs and lead fewer training courses. She wants to be more involved in using her mind.

Not all of her colleagues immediately welcome this plan enthusiastically because they would like to do the same. But her younger colleagues are eager to use her experience and ideas. Liz is better able to understand that sometimes her creative proposals were too innovative, resulting in resistance. Through trial and error Liz learns to focus more on what works well, an essential precondition if she is to find some form of balance in her inclination to be a perfectionist.

Finding ways to relax
Liz wants to participate more in sports and to force herself to do something that she finds pleasant at least one day a week. She realizes she needs to make a distinction between relaxing and working. She also continues to paint and look for other forms of creative expression to be better able to cope with her emotions.

To recap
The occupational physician and the Work and Organizational psychologist together discuss Liz's case.

Under her previous manager, Liz functioned well, but things went wrong when the new manager arrived. From the very beginning, Liz thought that this man was stupid and lazy. As a result, she then imposed her own vision upon him rather forcefully and became increasingly sarcastic about him. In her colorful description of her new manager you can see her huge observational capacities. It seems very likely that her manager felt threatened by her critical attitude from the start. Liz thought that he did not treat her with respect. She also blamed him for the fact that he took no action when her colleague left. Liz became increasingly compulsive, not only towards her manager but also with regard to her work. In her own assessment, her performance deteriorated. She felt that no one listened to her and engaged in a power struggle with her manager and finally became ill.

Because of her enthusiasm and drive, Liz lost control over herself and her work situation. This is a typical sign of someone being overstressed. Under these circumstances, occupational physicians often advise a brief period of rest to take a look at the work situation. This was followed by a phase of rationalization. By providing this analysis, the occupational physician tried to help her, but at the time Liz still would not accept that she was overstressed and even showed symptoms of burnout. After she received information about burnout and becoming overstressed, she was able to come up with a number of solutions and implement them.

It is striking that Liz seems to be very dependent upon the support of her manager. When she received support, she performed very well. But when she did not receive this support, her situation rapidly deteriorated. At that point she was no longer able to distinguish between what could reasonably be expected of her and what might be expected from her environment (her manager and colleagues). Instead of seeking support, she antagonized people and then also blamed herself because this was happening. The line between her work (what she does) and who she is, became increasingly vague and finally Liz became her emotions, instead of having emotions. During her recovery, Liz was greatly helped by her high giftedness. She is capable of clear analysis and astute observations. She is able to be emphatic and has a sense of humor, which means that she can quickly determine how and why things went the way they did. Liz was actually handicapped most by her own strong emotions. The greatest challenge Liz faced was to find a proper balance between thought and emotion.

We believe that her decision to become more involved in creative activities as a way to express her emotions, offers a good solution to help her find a greater balance in life. We want to focus mainly on asking Liz about everything she managed to achieve. With the help of a coach, Liz is perfectly capable of maintaining control over herself and her situation, but perhaps she needs some guidance for a while to help ensure that she retains some balance between her emotions and thoughts, between work and leisure, between what goes well and what could be improved and between what she can influence and what are the responsibilities of others. And perhaps Liz could also learn how she can iprove the way in which she deals with conflicts.

She has decided that, for the time being, she will not go and talk to her manager. Yet, such a discussion might be useful to discover what happened between them. Perhaps Liz could make one of her beautiful drawings or paintings about the subject...

2. I'll do it myself...

Jacob Swart is 41 years old and has worked at a university in various positions for the last 15 years, beginning as a teacher in economics. He excelled in developing teaching materials, but lacked effective teaching and communication skills (e.g. he often talked too much). Jacob is well respected in his department because of the quality of his teaching materials and his usually cheerful attitude.

Jacob organized regular social get-togethers at which he provided good food and where he told wonderful stories. In passing he would mention that in high school he took four additional courses, was an editor of the school paper and still felt bored. So, he said, he decided to read all the books in his father's library. "The things I learned there!" Jacob would say, laughing wickedly...

Strangely, Jacob was very gloomy on occasion and his colleagues couldn't get through to him at those times. He would sit at a table, alone, growling under his breath if anybody asked how he was doing, shuffled through the hallways and spent all day sitting at his computer, writing course materials. (According to Jacob, he needed to improve what his colleagues had written.) His coworkers expressed concern, but Jacob dismissed their worries and just kept working.

Four years ago, a position became available as a department head in a university agency focusing on educational reform, which would mean working with a number of other universities and a large company to develop interactive education materials. Jacob was very interested in the job. Although there were some concerns about his communication skills, Jacob was given the position because of his vast knowledge and his enthusiasm for the project.

Jacob currently heads a small group of researchers and advisors. His intelligence and hard work has gained him respect from his colleagues. Once again, he organizes popular get-togethers. However, Jacob cannot get along with one of his colleagues, Alice. Jacob thinks that she is not committed to the project and, as a result, does not fulfill her commitments. He complains about her to other colleagues, who do not know what to do. However, Jacob is reluctant to confront Alice directly.

Jacob's department is under significant pressure from the university board because this educational reform initiative is a prestigious project involving two other universities and a large company. A great deal of money is involved, and the project needs to show results at all costs. As a result of this pressure Jacob, in his turn, demands a lot from his employees. Although Jacob places value on creating a good atmosphere in his department, he is unhappy with the quality of work of his staff, also believing that their pace of work is much too slow. A number of his employees feel pressured because of Jacob's demanding standards. More than once Jacob has required his team to work through the weekend to complete a document. If they do not, Jacob finishes the project himself. Consequently, Jacob works at home most weekends and starts doing everything himself, including writing content.

Jacob's wife is troubled by his heavy workload and the effect it has on his health. He works late into the night, sleeps little, and no longer has time for other things. Increasingly, he withdraws from his wife and his colleagues, not even reacting to their expressions of concern.

Jacob just continues to work even harder. During meetings with the university's management, Jacob criticizes his colleagues and other departments, but he doesn't notice the lack of any positive response to his comments.

A number of employees confront Jacob, but every time they do that, he becomes more rigid in his attitude and interaction. Ultimately his staff assumes that Jacob will do everything himself anyway. Jacob expects written memos about everything, and he then goes through them with a red pencil. Everything is wrong in his judgment. And then Jacob usually rewrites the whole memo himself.

Finally, problems arise within the parent company of the prestigious project because Jacob can no longer deliver results on time. When financial problems emerge, university management has had enough. To his dismay Jacob is suspended. Believing that he is the only person actually delivering high quality results, he considers the suspension especially unjustified.

At the same time, he is experiencing physical problems and exhaustion. On his wife's advice he visits his family doctor, who advises him to see the university's occupational physician who diagnoses him as suffering from serious burnout and depression.

Analysis of the situation
Undoubtedly Jacob is gifted. He calls himself 'smart.'
He is an expert, quickly understands problems, contributes good solutions, works quickly, can generate good quality written materials, and is, when relaxed, very amiable. However, when Jacob is under pressure he falls into a series of behavioral pitfalls. He works even longer and harder, no longer listens to others, demands too much of himself and others, and is no longer approachable. At such times Jacob's wife cannot reach him, creating tension in the marriage. Jacob falls into a period of depression, as occasionally happens to gifted people.

Because of his strict focus on his work, Jacob doesn't realize that he doesn't 'connect' during his contacts with the university's management and the company, and blames others for the fact that parts of the project aren't ready. There is a clear gap between what Jacob thinks is good and his skills to communicate this to his environment. What he thinks is clearly agreed upon is not clear to others. The people around him say: "he doesn't track."

The suspension came as a bolt from the blue to Jacob. Despite the series of discussions with management leading up to this action, Jacob strongly believes it was wrong that he is the only one blamed for the project's failure. He doesn't understand why this is the case. In his mind, others are to blame. He decides to discuss the matter with the occupational physician.

This is the occupational physician's report:

Reflection on the situation

I know this organization well, so I can review with Jacob how all of this could have happened, from both his and the organization's perspective. I quickly recognize the symptoms of burnout and tell him a bit more about what burnout involves. *(See also the information chapter).* Jacob understands what I tell him and agrees with my diagnosis.

Because I believe that Jacob is depressed, I also discuss those findings with him. After our talk, I refer him to a psychotherapist. Jacob is also prescribed antidepressants (through his family doctor) and has a number of urgent conversations with his therapist. At these sessions Jacob discusses his childhood, which, the therapist concludes, is the root of many of his current problems.
(The limits of this book do not permit us to include an extensive report regarding this case.)

Jacob is now unable to work and this continues for about six months. During that time he talks to me every three weeks. In the meantime it becomes clear that his employer would prefer that Jacob starts to look for another job.

Jacob negotiates with his employer to receive facilities and support in searching for a new job. Eventually Jacob finds a career coach himself.

Below is a description of the guidance provided by the career coach.

Dealing with obstructive thoughts
During our first conversation Jacob tells me that he has arranged for transfer to another job through his former employer. That is the reason he contacts me. But actually he already has a plan. Jacob wants to pursue a master's degree in 'quality management'. He still disagrees with his suspension and is upset that the university didn't arrange another job for him. I do not understand Jacob's motivation to study quality management and what he expects of me. When I ask for clarification, Jacob comes up with a very convoluted story. After a while it becomes clear that he thinks he is suited for quality management because this will allow him to 'provide individual guidance'. He says he mainly needs my help to learn how to find another job, how to tackle the job search.

When I ask him whether we can take a step back and explore what he is really interested in, based on his experiences, he rejects this suggestion. He thinks he is already well informed about different courses and knows for himself what is best for him.
He already visits his therapist to discuss his life, so he doesn't want to duplicate that effort. Jacob only wants to talk to me about losing his job and especially how unjust that was. Jacob has a fair number of reasonable arguments for that. He does not talk about his anger.

Jacob tells me that he really enjoys hiking. I propose that we take a walk together in a nature park. Jacob likes that idea. I ask him to write down in advance what he wants to learn during the walk. Jacob says that he is willing to write something down "if it is necessary." Because Jacob knows that I am a biologist, he looks up the names of a few special plant species which he 'would like to see.' Not a word about himself. I decide to confront him on that during the hike.

Dealing with emotions

When starting the hike, Jacob immediately takes off at high speed. Even when I ask him to slow down, he stays a few meters ahead of me, sweat streaming down his face.
I ask him whether he always does that. "Yes," he says, not to push himself as much as possible (as I assume), but "because I just have a high speed."

When I don't say much, Jacob starts telling me a beautiful story about an earlier hike in the mountains with his wife. It is mainly about his wife, not about himself. He also describes a wonderful dinner in an Italian restaurant. That is how I learn that Jacob likes to cook and does it well. According to him he cooks much better than his wife.

I tell him that it strikes me that he is out front everywhere, literally and figuratively. I ask Jacob to walk behind me for a while. I take it easy, noticing that Jacob has a lot of trouble with holding back and following my pace. He asks if I could speed up a bit. When I say that I'm looking for his special plants, Jacob starts looking around for the first time. When eventually we find a meat-eating plant, he is enthusiastic.

Jacob proposes resting for a while at a beautiful spot and sits down on a bench, taking all kinds of wonderful things from his backpack. Home-baked apple pie, a cold pasta salad, everything nicely wrapped. The food is not just for him, but for me, too. Suddenly Jacob has all the time in the world. He likes the fact that I am pleasantly surprised.

I tell him that I think I have made contact with him for the first time. Jacob starts talking, sharing a great deal about his family, his parents and his own family. Jacob left home when he was 16 because of the tensions that existed between his parents. His mother was disabled, and his father was hardly ever home. His mother often yelled from her wheelchair and beat him when she had the chance.

Jacob describes his childhood in a cheerful way, but I think that it was nothing to laugh about. For example he calmly describes how he once was severely beaten by his father and was locked in the basement. And how he, being the oldest child, intervened in quarrels because otherwise they would get out of hand. That story, too, he tells with much laughter. I ask Jacob if that doesn't make him feel very sad. Jacob agrees, falling silent for a moment.

When he wants to start a new story, I ask him to look around and describe what he sees. It starts raining and we sit on the bench together under an umbrella. Jacob clearly feels less comfortable and wants to resume hiking. We look out over an endless field of partly burnt heather. It looks depressing in the rain. Jacob describes in detail what he sees.

When I ask him how he *feels* about the surroundings, he replies: "it is rather desolate here." I ask if that feeling is similar to how he feels about his life. Jacob immediately sees through my question and says, smiling: "Yes, sure..." After a long silence he adds: "You want to hear how things are, right?" I explain that understanding his feelings would help me to guide him more effectively. Jacob then talks about his anger around losing his job, his disappointment and the blow to his feelings of trust in management. He becomes more and more sad.

There are long periods of silence. Jacob sighs and is sad – until he opens his backpack again and this time produces a box of chocolates. Apparently Jacob wants to change the subject of our conversation. I suggest that he also discuss our hike with his therapist. And I then ask Jacob to describe the seven most beautiful moments in his life, and what he felt at those times.

In the meantime we have hiked quite a distance, with Jacob adjusting his speed to mine. But he still wants to choose the way himself. However, I notice that he knows exactly where we are. Jacob notes as an aside that he prefers to keep things under his own control. Jacob has no problem finding a bus stop and that is the end of our hike.

Motivation

During our next conversation Jacob reports that he discussed our hike with his therapist. He expressed a lot of sadness, he says, and it makes him depressed to relive the conversation. He asks if it is really necessary to go through all of this history in order to find a new job. I tell him that I am struck by the fact that the only contact between us occurred when we took a break on the bench. That he only noticed me being there when he looked around. And that we only had a real conversation about what really touched him then. That this emotion is the first step in finding a job that will really fit him. And that this is also a quest to discover what inspires him, who he is, what he can and cannot do and what problems he has.

Jacob starts discussing that with me. He does not agree with me, but eventually promises to cooperate.

Jacob has written a fine essay about the seven most beautiful moments in his life. He describes many moments with friends and his wife, on vacation or being together when he cooks tasty meals. Reading a number of American writers also gives him much pleasure. His stories include travel stories written with humor but which also are detached. And then there was that moment when he found a solution to a very difficult teaching problem. He has written a beautiful software program that worked. He is still proud of it.

To get a picture of what motivates Jacob, I ask him to draw a coat of arms, a 'signia' showing other people his true self. Jacob is to design this coat of arms using pictures and including rhyming poems. I give Jacob two weeks to finish it. Sighing, Jacob says that he cannot draw at all, but when I do not react, he feels that he has to go to work.

After two weeks we discuss the results. Jacob has drawn a gray little man and underneath it a rhyming poem with much self-mockery. He has added pictures of many books, and a bottle of wine. It appears that Jacob worked on his 'assignment' with the same snickering attitude he used when he told me his family history. He distances himself from himself, as it were. Jacob doesn't like my comments, but admits that "...there may be something in them".

A picture emerges based on his coat of arms. Jacob excels in finding solutions for difficult problems. He prefers doing that alone, by himself, without others. Jacob's choice to study quality management does not seem to fit what he really wants to do. Jacob also enjoys treating his friends, preferably by cooking complex recipes. But he intensely dislikes all kinds of meetings and consultations. And he is committed to producing work of a high quality.

Jacob thinks that he communicates well. When I explain that this is different from making contact, he looks surprised. We conclude that Jacob is good at talking about *content*, but that he is not effective in making his expectations clear and holding employees accountable. Also, asking others to help him is simply not part of his vocabulary. So it is logical that Jacob does everything by himself. Jacob has to learn much about these skills and practices.

Based on Jacob's stories about his most beautiful moments and his coat of arms, I ask if he has ever thought about opening his own restaurant. Jacob says he considers that too risky, but he has thought of opening his house to guests. When we continue talking about that vision, Jacob suggests he might want to do 'something for the hiking public.' He decides to outline a few good routes with attractive descriptions and to plan a wonderful evening dinner with a good glass of wine. He becomes enthusiastic as he talks.

In order to fulfill his intellectual needs, he will search for an innovative company where he can help identify solutions for complex problems. I ask him to write down his view of the future. Motivated, Jacob starts working!

Self-reflection
During our conversation Jacob becomes more aware of his sadness. Although he comes to understand how this influences his current situation, he tries to avoid feeling this sadness as much as possible.

He continues to find it hard to accept the 'failure' of his university project, especially failing to understand what his role was there. Jacob wanted to do everything himself, he could not hand off anything, demanded much from his environment, lost contact with his wife and finally lost contact with himself. Jacob did not feel his own limits and kept going until he reached burnout.
He is also unaware of the effects on others of the way he communicates. Only when I confront him with my own reactions does he stop and think about it. And he also discusses those themes in his therapy. It makes Jacob very uncertain.

Eventually he begins the journey to find out what really interests him. Another discovery for Jacob is the way he plays sports – hiking, rowing and biking, all activities involving speed. Jacob carries an odometer, and measures the time he is active. For example, when rowing, he counts the number of times he uses his oars. In short, sports are an effort. You do sports to achieve something, according to Jacob. And Jacob likes competing with other people, including his wife. As a result it is almost impossible to win when playing with Jacob and not everyone can take this.

Jacob begins to see the connection between his burnout and his behavior and understands the importance of the journey toward that which touches him emotionally.

After a couple of months and after reaching these insights, Jacob is able to start looking for what he wants to do next. In the meantime, he decides not to study quality management but switches to information management.

How to proceed?
During the journey with the career coach, Jacob decides to take the following actions:

Finding a new job
Jacob selects a number of help-wanted ads; we then discuss these jobs based on his motivation. Jacob wants to work for a research company involved in innovation. He is open to fields other than the information sciences.

When Jacob's first efforts to find a new job do not yield results, he relapses into despair, feeling worthless and discarded. Many old feelings surface which Jacob discusses with his therapist. After a few months Jacob finds a job, but this is one he likes less than he wanted.

Finding limits
Jacob himself expresses that he finds it hard to realize when he has reached his limits, either his physical or his psychological limits. Physically he goes all out. He only feels tired afterwards. Finding his psychological breaking point is even harder. Based on his description of the signals he received during the weeks before his burnout, he discovers cognitively what these signals are. But he ignored them. Now, Jacob is more aware of those signals and is committed to proceeding with greater awareness.

Relaxing
Jacob decides to take up golf after realizing how he behaves when doing sports. Golf is a game where you have to relax and yet you have to learn good techniques, he explains. He likes that and thinks that he may be less competitive when playing this game. He also decides he might enjoy sailing with his wife once in a while.

That will take him away from it all. And once again he wants to invite friends and to cook for them.

Voicing expectations and learning to negotiate
Jacob learns that his communication style is very indirect and does not make clear what he expects from other people. In his new job he begins to pay more attention to this, though he still finds confrontation difficult. He comes to see that he has high standards and therefore he prefers working with people who work the same way. Negotiating what is feasible is a new perspective for Jacob. He realizes he needs some practical training, though he does not want to take a course in this field. But Jacob says he now sees the need to choose a good coach in his new job.

Reconnecting with his wife
Jacob is bothered by the fact that he did not have time for his wife, when he was too busy with work. He now understands that his wife suffered. While he was home because of his burnout, he talked a lot with his wife. She provided much support and Jacob was very happy about that. His wife also joined him when he went to therapy. That provided both with many insights about the way they had treated each other. Jacob resolves to make more time for joint activities with his wife. He also decides to cook for his wife, which she really appreciates.

To recap
The occupational physician and the career coach together review Jacob's situation. These are their views.

The occupational physician
I saw that Jacob already showed many signs of burnout when he was still working. Burnout is the result of a disruption of the balance between work demands and personal needs.
In Jacob's example I saw that he experienced many demands because of a prestigious project he was working on. He wanted to deliver high-quality work and he had trouble delegating

work to others. This caused a disruption of the balance.
*(For a further explanation of nervous exhaustion and burnout
see the information chapter.)*

I think that gifted people are susceptible to burnout
because they tend to keep going. And they pay too little
attention to their bodies' signals indicating that they are
going too far. In Jacob's case, his manager suspended him
(see above) when the situation became impossible. Eventually they agreed on a transfer to another job.

Jacob was confronted with the high demands he put on
himself and his environment. Those demands contributed
to his burnout. He was forced to change his work style and
to find a better balance between his private and work life.
I expect that Jacob, after his painful experiences, will now
recognize the signals of burnout much earlier. In my opinion
the fact that he is gifted helped him gain insight into his situation and his own reactions, although mainly at the rational level. The story of his dealings with the coach gave me,
as an occupational physician, much insight.
I think that it will make it easier for me to recognize people
who can be helped through such a route, making it easier
for me to refer and motivate them. I myself gained yet
another example of the susceptibility for burnout in a gifted
employee from Jacob's situation.

It is important – not only for me as an occupational physician, but also for gifted people themselves – to recognize
and acknowledge the factors that may lead to burnout, so
that they can adjust earlier in the process and ask for guidance if necessary. In Jacob's case there was also a combination of burnout and depression. It is important to make
that diagnosis early in the process. In those cases medication might help to cure the symptoms of depression, making
the guidance more effective.

In addition, communication also plays a role *(see chapter 4).*

The career coach
In Jacob's situation his experiences when he was young
played an important role, too. As the oldest child in a family
with a disabled mother and an 'absent' father, Jacob took
on the responsibility for the whole family at an early age. He
tried to make the best of it in difficult circumstances.

That pattern also showed in his work. Jacob felt responsible
for everything and took on everybody's work. He was unable
to continue to do that during the prestigious university project. I can imagine that he, being so driven and involved,
was deeply disappointed in his employer. Jacob himself was
so focused on the contents of his work that he missed a lot
of the signals from his environment. His burnout forced him
to reflect on his actions, but – even harder for him – to feel
his anger and sadness. Jacob's survival strategy was working harder and laughing off his unpleasant experiences in
his youth.

Through the journey to discover what really motivates him
and through his therapy, he was able to get back in touch
with his feelings. It wasn't easy to win his trust, but when I
eventually succeeded, the discussions with Jacob were very
instructive. He always got to the bottom of things; he read
much and told fascinating stories. Many people who experience burnout are forced to think about that and to reorient
their work and their lives. Jacob did that. I think his journey
of discovery hasn't ended yet....

3. I spy with my little eye

Fifty-two year-old Samantha Smith has not worked outside her home for many years. After briefly studying at a vocational school, she married and quickly gave birth to three children. Samantha has been an active volunteer at her children's school and the local tennis club, where she served as the treasurer. In addition to caring for her children, who required a lot of attention, she took care of her mother and devoted a lot of time to her hobby, making quilts (something she does with dedication). Because her husband had a hectic business travel schedule, it was lucky that Samantha did not mind staying at home. There just wasn't time for a job. Raising her son Marc, the eldest, was especially time consuming, requiring her to spend a great deal of time with school advisors, psychologists, and personal tutors.
Ultimately, tests determined that Marc was gifted, but also exhibited some characteristics of autism. Samantha worked hard to make sure that he developed essential skills, especially social skills. She noticed that Marc and her husband shared similar traits, and this added more strain to the marriage. In order to save their marriage, Samantha proposed to her husband that they go to relationship therapy, but when he wasn't interested in trying to find help, Samantha was deeply disappointed. Not knowing what to do, she scheduled several visits with a psychologist by herself.

Samantha also wanted to go back to work, after the children left home. She applied for many positions, but her age and lack of work experience made it difficult to find work. Through a temporary job she ended up at a research company which conducted telephone surveys for scientific research. Initially she considered it just a way to get back to working, but she found she enjoyed the work. She worked energetically, learned quickly, and was able to work independently, all after only a short training period. She worked on average two afternoons and three evenings a week at the office.

After only a few weeks, Samantha began to notice numerous problems in the department, observing that the work wasn't done very well. Her colleagues did not pay attention to instructions. For example, she heard that many questions were asked in a suggestive way during the phone calls, which skewered the results of the research. In addition, she noticed that the information collected by her colleagues was often recorded incorrectly. She found many mistakes and became concerned that these errors would lead to incorrect results.

Another thing she found was that reimbursement procedures for travel expenses and employee insurance were unclear. When her supervisor could not come up with satisfactory answers to her questions, Samantha contacted the human resources department. Her supervisor was not pleased with that, concluding that Samantha was disloyal.

Samantha found the call center where she worked so noisy that she had difficulty conducting phone interviews. Her colleagues talked very loudly on their phones and amongst themselves. When she complained about the noise, colleagues yelled at her. Adding to her stress was the fact that after working for a few months, Samantha still had not been paid.

After four months she cannot take the stress any longer, she feels extremely tired and seeks help from her physician.

The doctor asks her about her work situation and advises her to reduce her hours. Samantha initially resists but a talk with her husband helps her decide to cut back on her evening schedule. Finding it hard to talk with her supervisor directly and hoping to avoid a confrontation, she leaves a letter on his desk informing him that from now on she will be able to work only one evening a week. She adds a list of the workplace problems she has observed. When her supervisor reads her letter, he gets very angry and he fires Samantha on the spot.

Samantha is horrified and very surprised at this response and asks for a meeting with her supervisor. She tells him she did not intend to criticize his management style. He criticizes her habit of making critical comments about everything – which she has done from the very start – and suggests she wants to change the rules. He tells her that she has communicated her concerns poorly and says her colleagues are bothered by the way she communicates. "We don't work this way. We don't play I spy with my little eye..." he says. He goes on to criticize her behavior, suggesting that she uses a high-pitched, shrill voice and is always making accusations. "As if everyone is wrong and only you, Samantha, do things correctly. If somebody complains about this, you only say: Can't you guys take criticism?"

Samantha is shocked – does she really act that way? After all, she only wants the work to be done well. She does not know what to say and goes home feeling bad. She immediately calls Cecile, a good friend, and starts crying. She had been so happy to go to work and now this has happened! What can she do? Cecile proposes that she and Samantha make a list of everything that occurred. They agree to meet at Cecile's house to talk things over. Samantha repeats the comments her boss made about her communication skills and that this was the reason for her being fired. She is still very angry about his criticism. When, to her dismay, Cecile says that she agrees with Samantha's boss, Samantha finds that very hard to take. Cecile describes several examples of this behavior. While Samantha does not like being criticized by Cecile in this way, she begins to realize the effect her own communication style has on others.

Cecile suggests that Samantha seek professional help, because, she has observed Samantha act toward her children and husband in the same way. When Samantha later asks her husband about it, he admits that her criticism really bothers him, both when they deal with the house or with his work. Samantha becomes very unhappy after hearing this feedback from her husband and good friend. Is she really such a bad person? Where did she go wrong? And how can she find her way back? She realizes that she does need to consult a professional, even though she maintains that she was in the right at her job.

Analysis of the situation
Samantha exhibits a number of characteristics typical of the gifted. Her quick and cutting analysis of people when things go wrong, her perfectionism, and her fierce reactions are characteristics that gifted people often share. Sensitivity to noise is another example. Moreover she shows no awareness of her own high standards and unforgiving nature.

Even though she is often correct, Samantha expresses her criticism very forcefully, not realizing that her colleagues and manager do not appreciate her style. When her manager and colleagues react harshly to her criticisms, she becomes angry, feeling wronged. She consistently blames others because she thinks she is right. Only by talking with her girlfriend does she understand how her communication style antagonizes everyone. Her husband also suffers under her reactions. And even worse, she was summarily fired because of her own actions!

Samantha presents her story to a Work and Organizational psychologist. Below is the psychologist's report.

Reflection on the situation
Samantha immediately fires away in the first session. Sharply and fiercely she explains at high speed her colleagues' irresponsibility, other work problems, the company being slow in paying her, and finally her abrupt firing. How is this possible? She suggests that several of her colleagues are just jealous because she understands everything so quickly and clearly.

I find it hard to interrupt Samantha and to ask why she thinks the problems are always somebody else's. Suddenly Samantha falls quiet. And she then relates her girlfriend's opinion that her firing might be the result of her own communication style. Samantha wants to hear more about this from an expert. And if the expert concludes that she has to change her way of communicating, she will need advice in what to do.

Dealing with obstructing thoughts
Samantha explains what happened at her job. She wonders why she is the only one to notice the problems at work and say something about them. Why did no one want to listen to her? I notice her accusatory attitude towards her manager and co-workers. Samantha clearly believes that her criteria for quality work are the only correct ones. And she expects the same from others. She is quite forceful about this. When I ask if there may be other ways to approach these problems, she becomes confused.
I observe several irrational thoughts behind her approach. Is it true that Samantha believes there is only one way to do things? And is it true that everything at her job must be done perfectly? Whoever disagrees with her is wrong, according to Samantha. She violently disagrees with me. We stop talking. I decide to go a step further. I tell her: "My impression is that you, Samantha, act like a prosecutor when communicating with your colleagues and your manager. This behavior gives the impression that you are always right and the others are completely wrong.

That is why you, in your opinion, have the right and duty to prosecute the others and blame them without indicating what needs to change." *(This theme will also be discussed in chapter 8.)* Samantha blushes. Does she really come across as believing that? That isn't what she wants at all.

I wonder if I have been too confronting. That is why I ask her what she was thinking when she wrote to her supervisor and listed everything that was wrong in the organization. Samantha explains what she was thinking:
- Why does nobody understand that I am right?
- Why do they always oppose me?
- I can't take this anymore.

I suggest that her comments reveal a few irrational thoughts, namely:
- I must be right.
- My opinion is the best one.
- Disaster will strike if I don't say anything, and I can't bear that.

We discuss whether her thoughts fit with reality. Samantha explains that nobody wants to admit that she was right. When I press her on this, it turns out that one of her colleagues did think Samantha had a good point, but didn't communicate it well. It also turns out that Samantha was not sabotaged. Her manager was indeed angry about her going to the human resources department. Samantha is very tired and depressed after all the 'stuff' at work, but she does like the work itself. What would have happened if she had stayed quiet? What if she had decided she could not take it anymore?

Samantha has a few thoughts that are a bit more nuanced. She tends to look at everything very critically. She does re-gister positive signals, but she does not 'save' them. Our conversation reveals that Samantha thinks she always loses in a discussion. That she often feels that people do not listen to her. She suddenly remembers that she felt the same way, when she was young and lived at home and discussed things with her father. He, too, always knew better. She is shocked to realize that she has adopted several character traits of her father's that she hated.

Later, we discuss her 'perfectionism' in other areas and their positive and negative points. For example: quilts must be exactly so and the edges must be perfectly finished and not bunch up. When she served on the board of an organization, she was always the treasurer. You could be sure that the books were correct, to the penny. I ask about her family interactions. Samantha admits that she often reacts the same way with her family, leading to unpleasant situations. She usually focuses on what her husband and children do wrong. She now begins to realize that her usual reactions are disturbing.

What does it mean to do things as well as Samantha? She explains that this often leads to fighting. She is very persistent when she thinks she is right and finds it hard to let go of situations like that. The issues keep replaying in her head. Always thinking that she *has to succeed* causes much stress. Sometimes she fears that she just cannot do it. She discovers that she has serious feelings of inferiority. Samantha admits to experiencing low self-esteem if people do not listen to her, causing anger and depression. At those times she thinks she does not matter at all to other people.

Suddenly, the penny drops and a light comes on. A pattern emerges. Samantha has little self-confidence. In order to hide this, she harshly attacks others, not realizing that this will result in attacks on her. She finds those attacks horrible experiences and reacts very emotionally.

I tell her that I observe in her many of the characteristics of gifted people.
There may be a connection between her work problems and the characteristics of her high intelligence. The fact that she may be gifted surprises her. She has observed this in

her son, but thought he inherited those traits from his father. When I tell her that her analytical skills, ability to see weaknesses, her perfectionism, and sensitivity to sound, may all be linked to being gifted, she is very surprised. With her inferior school education she never considered herself gifted. It will be good for her to read something about this phenomenon. She starts reading everything she can lay her hands on. At the next meeting she gives me an extensive lecture about high giftedness including all the possible problems that this can create for adults!

Dealing with emotions

I observe that Samantha becomes irritated and angry very quickly. Such behavior, and not knowing how to deal with her emotions, paralyzes her. She sometimes feels deeply hurt, and starts acting like a victim ("I try to make everything better here and they don't want to listen to me...") At those times she feels pathetic, thinking nobody likes her. When I ask her to select a picture matching her feelings she picks out a card with a duck being attacked from behind by a swan. During that exercise she becomes very emotional. She says that she feels small, afraid of being attacked suddenly and wants to disappear under water to escape. She admits to being afraid of her emotions, thinking she does not dare feel her sadness, and instead uses attacking language that is not understood by others.

By blaming others and by attacking them she does not have to experience feelings of powerlessness and failure. By 'diving under water' she is able to ignore the feelings of being powerless that she does not know how to handle.

Samantha is happy to understand the reasons for her emotional reactions. The possibility that she may be gifted provides much relief. But, she still does not know how to change her behavior.

We do some role-playing where Samantha plays the role of her manager, and I play Samantha, while pushing things a little. Samantha does not manage to make me see things reasonably, because I do not listen while feeling angry about everything that is wrong in the organization. She starts giggling nervously and says: "Oh dear, do I really do that so badly? If so, then I understand why Brent (her supervisor) found me so insufferable. Cecile, my girlfriend, showed me the same thing, and I was so shocked that I arranged these conversations with you."

Then she abruptly turns very sad. She suddenly remembers an episode with her son when she attacked him so fiercely that he became quite upset. At the time she had been shocked, but only now does she realize how she had touched him. She finally realizes the impact her roughness can have on others, and she becomes sad. She understands now that she has something to gain by relaxing her standards and learning to deal with her emotions of anger and shame about her failure. Samantha also profits from our communication exercises. For example, we practice how to raise things that she disagrees with and how to negotiate. We practice specific situations that bother her. I give her training materials. At my request, Samantha describes her personal disaster scenario: what will happen if things go differently? Will disaster strike? Which alternatives can you find to solve the same problem? Samantha finds that hard to do. She immediately feels as if she fails if she does not succeed right away.

When we start working with pictures and metaphors she easily adapts to them. This approach helps her to think about alternatives. Next, we do some negotiation exercise sessions. When dealing with concrete items, Samantha does very well. When dealing with her personal feelings, she sometimes shuts down completely, but she improves after more conversations and role-playing. Every time we meet, we discuss the thoughts that present new obstacles and her related feelings. Her insights help her identify alternatives to her typical behavioral patterns, solutions that she can find herself.

Motivation

After six sessions Samantha progresses to the point that she wants to do something with her giftedness. She takes a test and is very proud when she indeed scores highly. She considers starting a course in finance at an Internet college. If she enjoys that, and it works out, she will start looking for what she wants to do next. In addition, she considers becoming a math's tutor at the school her children attend.

As I learned through dealing with Samantha, she acts immediately. First we discuss Samantha's real interests. Based on the core quadrant model, we work out her qualities and challenges. I ask her to complete it together with her husband and her girlfriend Cecile.

Core quality model

The core quality model is based on four approaches: core qualities (characteristics), problems (excessive characteristics), challenges (points to be worked on, positive opposite of problems), and allergies (irritations). Many characteristics ('core qualities') become problems when they grow excessive. A person with the characteristic 'helpfulness' can have the problem 'meddlesomeness.' The challenge for this person is to let go in certain cases. The distortion of the challenge 'letting go' is called the allergy. In this case, indifference is the allergy of the helpful person.

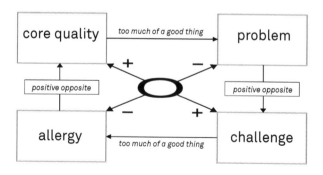

The core quality model is easy to use in our practice because of its simplicity. Unpleasant characteristics can be stated clearly, but not in a confrontational way. Putting them in the framework of 'too much of a good thing' makes the 'good' or 'well meant' characteristic visible. Next, the challenge shows the employee's development. Mutual irritations can almost always be named as allergies.
Based on Ofman, 2001, http://mijnkernkwaliteiten.nl/corequalities/whatarecorequalities.html

Samantha starts working with this model and masters it quickly, which pleases her immensely.
Samantha is very creative, as she shows when filling out her core qualities. Her creativity also shows in her quilting and patchwork and in designing clothes. She creates new patterns and then puts them on her website. I am concerned about her interest in studying finance. Samantha tells me that she is very exact and therefore likes doing things with numbers. In addition, finance connects well with her high school education. "Are you afraid you would fail if you were to do something other than finance?" I ask her. She thinks about that.

During our next session she says that her heart is not really in finance, but that she thinks it will be useful to get an additional certification. Her heart really is into designing wall hangings and clothing. She wants to make more free-form wall hangings, and is already collecting all kinds of cloth patches to make a piece using the theme 'water.' She also considers opening her own clothing business. And finally she also wants to study literature, because she is very fond of reading. Eventually she decides to study literature and make free-form wall hangings. She plans to sell them so that she will have her own source of income. She has done that before with her patchwork quilts. She postpones starting her own clothing business because that would require investing a lot of money.

How to proceed?

Through her conversations with the psychologist Samantha gains an excellent insight into her reactions and those of others to the way she does things. She wants to learn more about communicating. She also enthusiastically starts a study course that she really enjoys and makes wall hangings as an outlet for her creativity. She decides that she still has a lot to work on.

Training in negotiating, assertiveness and reframing
Because Samantha becomes judgmental so quickly, she decides to sign up for a course in rephrasing and negotiating skills. This course will teach her to rephrase her criticism into a request. This technique is also useful when negotiating and will provide her with more opportunities to look for alternatives. She hopes that this will teach her to put into perspective her first reaction or urge that there is only one way to do things – hers. Because she finds it especially hard to stand up for herself in a constructive way, assertiveness training will also be useful for her. This will teach Samantha to say what she wants and needs in a less aggressive way while communicating with others.

Relationship therapy
In the meantime her relationship with her husband has greatly improved. The contact with the children also improves. Her son recently told her: "Mom, you're doing very well! We can finally just talk with you! You no longer get angry about everything." She knows that there are still a number of obstacles to be cleared in her relationship with her husband. Her husband also wants that because he sees that Samantha has quieted down considerably. She now looks at her own behavior and does not blame everything on him anymore.

A new job?
Samantha really wants to work again. She wants to do something with gifted children, but first she wants to take the steps that are 'necessary', such as improving her

relationship with her husband and learning how to deal with her anger and depression. She also wants to start her wall hangings business and literature studies. In her enthusiasm Samantha finds it hard not to start everything all at once.

To recap
The psychologist discusses her contact with Samantha in her peer group of professionals. This is her story.

What I really liked about Samantha was her eagerness to learn and how quickly she grasped things. This was very stimulating to me. Harder to deal with were her fierceness and her tenacity. Sometimes it seemed that she was a kind of closed book. At those times nothing could get in. That is why in those situations I chose provocation, and luckily that worked well.
I think Samantha was going through a very hard time when she came to me. She had just been fired from the job that she had started with so much enthusiasm. In addition, she was in a relationship that threatened to go off the tracks and she had much self-doubt that she dealt with by criticizing everything and everybody. Through my confrontations and our role-playing Samantha started thinking about what she wanted instead of what she didn't want. Recognizing that she was gifted helped her greatly. That showed her behavior in a very different light. Our analysis of her emotions and her irrational thoughts gave her much insight. It was good that she understood everything so well and also started working with it. Her passion to learn something from these experiences increased the chances that she will do much better in her next job.

Working with pictures also helped Samantha to understand her emotions. For people who are more geared toward sounds, music can also be a way to be able to feel. Writing rhymes and poems also may help as this all calls on the 'feeling' part of the brain. I think that she still has quite a way to go in the relationship with her husband. But because they now both want to improve the situation, I think chances of success are good.

4. I don't belong

Vincent White is a 38-year-old lawyer who works as a policy advisor in the Environmental Affairs Division at the Dutch Department of Infrastructure and Environment. He finds his work enormously interesting, reads everything he can find on the topic of environmental law and speaks about these issues passionately. He often becomes deeply involved in his work, especially when he works as the project leader on special projects.

During discussions in his department, when difficult and complicated items are discussed, he immediately identifies the issues and provides smart solutions. However, he notices that his colleagues take much more time to grasp the problem and don't understand what he is talking about. When they agree on what to do, he fulfills his part quickly and well. But his colleagues first call other people, endlessly research and confer with each other, and are generally very slow in providing their input. Always late! This irritates him immensely. The last time this happened, he really exploded and blurted out that he could not understand why his colleague, William, always needed so much time. This incenses William and other colleagues, especially because they think careful research takes a long time. They say Vincent always wants to do what he is convinced is best. And that he acts as if his approach is the only and best solution. They find him immensely arrogant. Maybe he should take a less self-righteous attitude, they think....

Vincent begins to notice that he is ignored more and more when practical jokes are made in the department. Are these jokes about him? And he notices also that his colleagues increasingly avoid him and don't say anything when he comes in, especially when they talk amongst themselves about their weekends. Actually he admits he is not at all interested in their lives and he probably shows it. He prefers a good conversation about the latest research on gas emissions, but, of course, that is not what people talk about around the water cooler. He would prefer to talk about that rather than talk about wives, children, soccer, and cars....

He feels that he is becoming the odd one out. But when his manager reports during his evaluation that Vincent's colleagues call him antisocial, aggressive, arrogant, dominant, and socially handicapped, he finds that an unwelcome surprise. His supervisor asks Vincent to try to become a better colleague, but Vincent doesn't understand exactly what that means. He says that he always looks for discussions while working on his projects and works hard to finish them on time and well. His supervisor agrees, but says that he creates a lot of resistance amongst his colleagues by the way in which he approaches matters. Maybe he should reflect on this.

Vincent does that, in part because he realizes that things aren't going that well in his private life either. Recently his girlfriend broke up with him, and Vincent doesn't really know why. Since then he avoids all kinds of social situations, like birthdays, gatherings and parties even more than he used to. Usually there is not much to do or say at these occasions, he thinks. He doesn't want to go out anymore, and certainly he doesn't want to attend events when he has to go all by himself. He'd rather read a good professional journal or a book.

Analysis of the situation

Vincent works with enthusiasm and does great work, technically. He quickly notices connections amongst other environmental laws and easily understands difficult materials. He expects similar high professional standards from his colleagues, but notices that they work much slower than he does. Vincent doesn't understand what they think is so difficult. The way he sees it, they talk way too much about irrelevant things, like personal affairs. Calling his colleagues to account for being late or not meeting his standards, creates a lot of irritation.

Through the discussion with his supervisor, Vincent learns that his colleagues increasingly resent him. He feels lonely and shut out. He notices that this causes him to feel increasingly uncertain of himself. This shows both at work and in his private life. This is the reason he avoids social situations, by not going out for drinks with his colleagues, birthdays, and events.

Vincent doesn't realize that his standards are much higher than average. This leads to a lack of understanding by others and to communication problems with his colleagues. This is a well-known phenomenon that occurs often in gifted people.

After having a discussion with his supervisor about his working style, Vincent realizes that he has a problem in his approach to life. While he still believes the main fault lies with his colleagues, Vincent does acknowledge that he has problems in his private life. His girlfriend recently decided to end their relationship. He doesn't know what to do about that, and he is unhappy. He wants to know what happened, but he doesn't know how to find out.

After hesitating for a long time, he discusses this with a good friend who advises him to speak to a psychologist. This friend thinks that Vincent is gifted and knows a psychologist with experience in counseling gifted people. Initially Vincent doesn't like the idea, but when he also starts to experience headaches, he sets up a meeting with the psychologist.

Reflection on the situation

Vincent explains the situation. Below is a report of the counseling process, as told by the psychologist.

Dealing with obstructive thoughts

Vincent tells me that, before he joined the Department of Infrastructure and Environment, he worked for the local government as an environmental policy advisor. Already then did he encounter similar problems, and that was the reason he applied for a job at the Department. He had expected the level of abstraction to be higher there. He was really disappointed to find that there were only a few colleagues he could really talk to.

Together we conclude that Vincent has rather high expectations of his working environment. I am also struck by his pointed judgments about his colleagues. His irrational thought behind this might be: "Everything has to go exactly the way I want it to go. If that doesn't happen, I feel unappreciated and shut out." Vincent thinks that he is blamed for every stupid document his colleagues produce. He then feels stupid and ridiculous. And he doesn't want to be seen as one of the stupid people.

What does Vincent think is stupid? He thinks documents are stupid if they are not logically laid out and are not suported by arguments and documentation. That is not the way to provide good policy advice, he thinks. He usually writes his policy notes at home where he isn't distracted. When I ask him whether his advice is always accepted, Vincent acknowledges that this isn't the case. He is frequently told that he doesn't consult others either in advance with his client(s), or with other departments or target audiences. Vincent hates group meetings.

We explore the meaning of departmental happy hour get-togethers and the personal events that he hates so much. When we talk, much old pain emerges. Vincent says that as a child he was often ridiculed during parties because he was always first, won many of the games and was way too serious. One time the children made a fool of him and threw him in the swimming pool with all his clothes on. This memory makes him really sad and he understands that it still plays an important part in his life.

I tell Vincent I see a number of characteristics showing that he is gifted. He thinks and associates quickly, switching from a strategic to a concrete level and strongly focuses on content. Vincent is not really surprised by that, he just hadn't made the connection with the harassment at school. He is also not trained in thinking and communicating at relationship levels *(see next paragraph)*.

He had always thought that his advice was rejected because he hadn't included everything.

Dealing with emotions
When Vincent delves more into himself during our conversations, he feels his anger, frustration, confusion, and sadness. He is really bothered by his colleagues ("they often don't know what they're talking about"), blames them for his being shut out ("they don't take me seriously"), but also that it is very sad ("I feel so lonely"). Through connecting with his earlier experiences Vincent can now better feel his emotions and better understand them. At children's parties he felt shut out and at school they thought he was a showoff. That is why he started feeling like an outsider already at a young age. This is a horrible feeling and that is the reason he started to avoid group meetings. Especially when these meetings are not about his field of expertise, Vincent does not know what to do and how to join in.

After gaining these insights I ask him to go to a friend's birthday party and to write down his experiences. Vincent returns with a very extensive report in which he precisely describes the party, the people, what they said, etc. But he also describes his own fear and the uncertainties he still feels. But because he now has more insight into his own emotions, he also sees how he can deal with this better.

At a second social event he attends, he says that he first walked around a bit and listened to what people were talking about. At one place the conversation was about somebody's work. He joined the group and heard a pediatrician talk about his experiences in the hospital.
He found this interesting and started talking with the people in the group. This was not easy for him, but he did notice that he grasped the situation and was able to join in the conversation. After he returned home he wrote down his emotions at the various stages of the party. This homework resulted in a good analysis of his feelings. But it was still from a distance, more written as an observer than as an experience.

We work on this in the next session. I notice that Vincent can express his feelings very well. We discuss the situation regarding his girlfriend. She had told him a number of times that she was not happy with the relationship. Initially Vincent reacted defensively: "This isn't my fault, is it?" Next he suggested going and doing something together. This seemed to him a good solution for his girlfriend's problem. She reacted by becoming very angry and telling him that he hadn't listened at all. And she despised his whining. Vincent had no clue what she was talking about. His girlfriend wanted to feel 'emotionally understood.' Vincent thought he did understand her, but she said that wasn't true. "Talking to him was like talking to a wall," she said and she didn't want this anymore. This sounds to me like communicating at different levels and not like connecting on a relationship level.

Content and Relationship level
When communicating with others we can send messages at a content level and at a relationship level. When communicating on a content level, we deal with transferring concrete content information. At a relationship level we deal with *how* a message must be interpreted and what the relationships are between

the people concerned. Often a message at content level is simultaneously sent at the relationship level. It is good to clarify not just the content, but also the relationship aspects of the communication. To do this it is necessary to call the other person to account, or to question him/her about the way he/she communicates. Then we don't discuss the message's contents, but its underlying significance and the relational side. So we communicate about the communication. This is called meta-communication.

From: Jackson, Beavin & Watzlawick, 1991.

Vincent admits that he never asked what his girlfriend meant with her questions for him. He also didn't ask what the relationship meant to his girlfriend, or to himself. He asks me to give some examples and to work with him. He confesses that he thinks that I (the psychologist) 'still have something to say.' Apparently he hadn't expected that.

Motivation
Vincent now realizes that because of his being gifted, he has achieved exactly the opposite of what he really wants, namely, feeling accepted and valued. That brings us to his motivation. What does he really want?

Vincent wants a job where he can express his intelligence. He finds his current job very interesting, offering him many challenges. He especially likes his projects because they impose deadlines, making the work exciting. However, what he expects from others is that they work just as fast and as driven as he. In this conversation I ask Vincent to paint a picture of this ideal. It turns out to be a kind of air balloon but without gas, because he just invented something new. We continue working with this picture.
Do all balloonists like this? "No," Vincent thinks, "I'm sure they also find it scary because he's the only one who knows about the invention." So we try to find what he can contribute to make it as much fun as possible for the other balloonists, too. This gives Vincent new energy.

He likes looking at ideas and projects in different ways and discovers there are other challenges, in which he can use his ability to quickly switch sides and to see connections.

As for his own needs, Vincent realizes that his colleagues are also important to him. He wants to be part of every-thing, in whatever way, and he doesn't want to be seen as an outsider. Some colleagues also made very good sugges-tions about how to have his advice accepted. Or how you can hold a meeting with all people working on the project, without this descending into 'just chatting.' He especially likes working with his colleagues in an Environmental Steering Group.

Self-reflection
Through our conversations Vincent gains more insight into his weak spots that show when he works with others. He is very content-focused. Up to now he never realized there might be a challenge in getting his colleagues to work with him and to look at what they think about the meaning of the work they do. He now also understands a bit more about their reactions. One of his colleagues once told him that they felt belittled by him. If he could better connect, e.g. by posing questions instead of immediately giving his own answer and (the only correct) solutions, he might have a significantly higher value for his department and elsewhere. It then becomes not a matter of accusing others that they don't live up to the agreements, but looking for a connec-tion, finding solutions together – solutions that in addition to being innovative can also be executed by everybody. Vincent will suggest to his colleagues that he will research the complicated tasks.

But he wonders how to do this. His colleagues now consider him arrogant and conceited. And Vincent himself needs his colleagues' trust and the space to do things differently. We look for strategies on how Vincent may reconnect with his colleagues. In addition, we also discuss his private life where he has shown similar bad communication skills.

How to proceed?

Because of Vincent's new insights through the discussions with the psychologist, a number of possible solutions present themselves. Vincent plans to do the following:

Conversation with his supervisor

Vincent wants to keep his current position because he likes the work and finds it challenging. He considers participating in the steering group and wants to discuss this with his supervisor. Through his conversations with the psychologist he realizes that his colleagues may also be a source of inspiration. In addition, his colleagues might also profit from his solid knowledge and his passion to research subjects thoroughly. Vincent now wants to be more positive and cooperative. He also has become more aware of his (too) high expectations regarding his colleagues and his aversion to small talk. But he wants to maintain his own drive and he wants appreciation and recognition from the organization. He plans to discuss all of this with his supervisor. What are the opportunities, what are the limitations? What can he contribute? And how can he reconnect with his colleagues? While at the same time getting them to allow him to work the way he wants to work. Vincent gets along reasonably well with his supervisor and hopes that as a result of this conversation he will receive more support for his 'new' behavior.

Working towards better cooperation with colleagues

Vincent now realizes that because of his being gifted, he analyzes, observes, and makes connections much faster and more accurately. Instead of expecting others to do the same, it would be better to 'offer' his talent instead of (as he has done up to now) pressing it on others and demanding others to work the same way. Through the association exercise of the air balloon, he also understands that he sometimes drifts away, that other people cannot keep up with him and find it annoying to have to depend on his knowledge and skills. He realizes that this requires him to take other people's opinions and routines into account and that he shouldn't always have his opinion at the ready. Vincent has no idea what they expected from him during the cooperation, and what they enjoyed. Now he is going to ask them that, with his supervisor's help.

Dealing with difficult colleagues may turn into a new challenge but also demands guidance for Vincent, for example through a coach who can help him evaluate the way he works with his colleagues, can discuss his reasoning, and can help him to work through his emotions. For Vincent this will mean that he has to look for a balance between adapting and innovating.

Conversation with his former girlfriend
Expanding on his experiences at work, Vincent decides to talk with his former girlfriend. He finds this very painful, but realizes that he can learn a lot from this conversation. We discuss what Vincent experiences as painful. This turns out to be especially the 'rejection' and his fear of 'not being good enough'. Here, too, earlier experiences with his father and friendships play a role.

To recap
The psychologist discusses Vincent's case with a friend who is an occupational physician. Below is a summary of their conversation.

We (the psychologist and occupational physician) think Vincent initially reacted very cognitively to his situation, like many gifted people do. In addition, he also tends to blame others *(this is called 'external locus of control' and is further explained in chapter 7)*. He was shocked by his experiences in his private life and by the conversation with his supervisor about his functioning. He started looking at the similarities in these two situations. His initiative to talk to a psychologist shows courage and the understanding that 'something needs to be done.' This intrinsic motivation increases the chances that there will be real change.

Vincent observes intensely, can describe well what others do, what others say, and what he does and says himself, but this still doesn't provide a balance in his own emotions. It is important to pay attention to gaining insight in connections with earlier experiences relating to his current reactions, emotions and behavior, we think.

The psychologist

My attention focused on better use of his talents combined with thinking more about his feelings and accepting and learning to deal with them. In addition, Vincent and I in our conversations worked on the way Vincent communicates with his environment (work and private life). By investigating the different aspects of communications, Vincent now has more tools available to continue working on this. After all my conversations with Vincent, I expect that he will begin to enjoy learning more about how to switch between content and relationship levels. After all, this appeals to his talent to quickly see connections, and to his great powers of observation.

5. Is this what I really want?

When Kitty den Hollander graduated from university with a major in mathematics at the age of 22, she faced a number of important choices in her life.
The youngest of three children, Kitty showed evidence of being gifted at an early age. Her sister Sandra, five years older, and her brother Bob, one year older, were also smart. But Kitty was always different. When her brother Bob learned to read, Kitty immediately learned to read, too, and they soon became real pals in everything, sometimes leaving her sister Sandra feeling shut out. Because of a five-year age difference, this seldom led to serious problems, but it did cause a strain in their relationship, which is evident even today. Kitty did well in school, until seventh grade, when she began to experience academic and social problems; she retreated into herself and for a long time didn't like going to school. Her teacher recognized in Kitty the characteristics of a highly intelligent person and sought confirmation through the school advisory service. Kitty was tested and it turned out she was indeed highly intelligent.

The school psychologist offered Kitty's teachers and parents practical tips to support her development. For example, Kitty was given the opportunity to read at a higher grade level. She was also given extra assignments, working in the school library where she helped to modernize the system used to loan out books. Kitty responded well to these arrangements and went to school with pleasure again. She made more friends and started music lessons, quickly showing a real talent for the violin. Playing music allowed Kitty to release her energy. She soon joined a youth orchestra and later became an orchestra leader.

At home, Kitty's parents gave her the freedom to pursue her interests, but they were a bit controlling. Kitty did well in sciences in high school, so her parents pushed her to study mathematics. However, she was more interested in attending a school of music. Her parents insisted, even going so far as telling her which university they preferred and even the sorority they felt would best suit Kitty. Wanting to please her parents, she gave in to their requests. Kitty began to study pure mathematics and commuted between her hometown and the nearby university so that she could continue to live at home.

During her studies, Kitty felt increasingly uncertain and sometimes even slightly depressed. She started fighting with her mother. She wanted to go to parties at night in her university town, but her parents thought that would be dangerous. As a result she had little contact with her fellow students.

Kitty finished her degree within the expected time and continued playing in the orchestra, greatly enjoying that. She found a series of summer jobs. But problems emerged during her jobs because she often spoke up and interfered in things she thought weren't done well. Neither her colleagues nor the manager appreciated her advice, and this often resulted in conflicts.

After graduation, Kitty started looking for a fulltime job. She saw an ad for a position as a PhD student to work on a dissertation that complemented her degree, a very theoretical subject in numerical mathematics. Her parents were very enthusiastic; they thought this was a good way to start her career. Kitty herself wasn't really happy, though. She had nightmares, waking up in a sweat, feeling as if she was suffocating. She wondered whether this job was what *she* wanted – or was it her parents' choice?

Now Kitty discusses her dilemma with one of her girl-friends, who studies psychology and sees how she struggles. Her friend advises her to postpone making the decision for a while, because this is truly an important moment in her life and to ask for help.her girlfriend has recently heard about a special workshop that helps smart people make good life choices and work on their careers. She thinks that this is what Kitty needs.

Analysis of the situation

Kitty is gifted, which helped her finish school and college on schedule. On the other hand, her high intelligence created problems like her unhappiness in high school and conflicts with supervisors and colleagues. The fact that Kitty readily accepted her parents' preferences of what and where to study and what sorority to join, showed that Kitty ignored her own wishes and dreams. She had never learned how to want something for herself.

Kitty is an example of someone who unerringly feels how she can serve others, especially her parents, but she then ignores her own wishes and dreams (showing a desire to please). Neihart (1999) noted that gifted adolescents often show the traits of perfectionism and competitiveness (in Kitty's case, these traits are less recognizable), have a strong drive to please their parents and are subjected to high expectations by parents. Miller (1979) also wrote about gifted children who understand what the parents expect, but if they follow those wishes, it negates their own feelings.

How can she change this behavioral pattern, now that she is choosing her first job?

Reflection on the situation

Kitty starts looking for jobs on the Internet, but finds nothing of interest. She does find a notice about career counseling for gifted people, a career adventure, aimed at very intelligent people who have not learned how to make choices based on their feelings. That adventure appeals to her.

She learns that the program involves spending a day in nature and completing several assignments, with a follow-up meeting three weeks later. She hesitates, thinking it sounds vague and that she is too young for that. However, Kitty knows that she has to do something and finally decides to register. Her parents are not willing to pay for it, but Kitty decides it will be worth it.

After the event, she does not think she got everything possible out of it. At her request, she meets with one of the counselors of the program and tells him her story.

Kitty says:
"I was sent into the woods with a number of other people with a rather vague assignment. I looked around and did not really know what I had to do. I asked Harry what he thought; he wasn't too sure either. I really didn't see the use of it at that point, but I thought that would disappoint my counselors and the others. So I decided to do the assignment as well as I could. I was afraid that otherwise I would create all kinds of confusion and that the others would find me a boring whiner. It was only after the whole thing was over that I questioned what I had really achieved out there in the woods. I had only been working on things that others expected of me and I wanted to be liked. But I didn't do what I really wanted to do. I was really shocked by that. That's what I always had done up to that point: doing what others wanted, not what *I* wanted... I did that even when choosing my field of study ... So I did not get everything available out of it. I thought: can I have a do-over?"

Dealing with obstructing thoughts
The career coach says:
This story demonstrates that Kitty has a number of irrational thoughts that keep her from making her own choices. Irrational thoughts contain an exaggerated 'must' and impose unreasonable demands on yourself or others.

For Kitty, they are the following thoughts:
- Everybody must like me, value me, think the best of me and love me.
- I must always be concerned about others.

Dealing with emotions
In general, the six categories of basic emotions are: anger, disgust, fear, happiness, sadness and surprise. Gifted people show many nuances in this range of feelings, but sometimes lose touch with their own feelings and emotions because of the situation in which they find themselves or where their thoughts lead them. Or they start fantasizing about what others think of them or what disasters could happen. Their feelings are negative, causing them to lose their inspiration, willpower and passion.

This story clearly shows that Kitty finds it very hard to deal with her emotions. She is afraid to say what she thinks and feels, because she is afraid others will then find her a boring nag. She also does not dare cry and so she hides her sadness and feelings of being hemmed in.

In conversations with a career coach (from the career adventure), Kitty reconnects with her feelings.

The career coach says:
"I ask Kitty how she felt during the assignment in the woods. She explains that she always becomes uncertain when she receives assignments that are not clear. This makes her confront herself. In these circumstances she wants to cry, but usually manages to set that feeling aside. She does think the stories told by other people are very

interesting and she listens to them a lot. She also likes being outside all day, despite the cold. She had never really done anything like that before going on that trip.

I ask her what happened after her adventure in the woods. Kitty explains that she took the PhD student position and started a training period. Her supervisor there is an unmarried woman who has been working there for thirty years. The supervisor is not an unkind person, but this person is fairly confrontational for Kitty. Kitty wonders if that will be her future too. Kitty suddenly realizes she made the wrong decision. She is slowly dying there, but quickly pushes that feeling away. She is afraid of her own feelings. After all, she is not allowed to dislike her job at the university, is she?"

Kitty's career coach proposes participating in a forestry project in Scotland. In such a completely different environment, where she will perform physical work, she may be able to figure out what is bothering her and what leads her to choose a job she doesn't really like.

After this conversation, Kitty runs into her cousin Caroline on the train on her way home. Caroline has always led a rather wild life. They lost touch over the years. When they meet Kitty and Caroline catch up, talking about things they remember from the past. Caroline says: "When I used to visit you at home, your mother said that she thought I was a bit too free and also impertinent. That 'her Kitty' was not like that at all. Later, I was talking about something, that you apparently weren't allowed to hear and then she asked me to shut my mouth. I said: "Shut your own mouth." Your mother really blew up at that! I always remembered that. I believe that afterwards I was no longer welcome at your house." This story shocks Kitty. She suddenly remembers that her mother always had an excuse why Caroline was no longer allowed to visit. Kitty thinks Caroline is impertinent, but you can always have a good laugh with her.

Kitty realizes that her mother has really ruled her life and that she herself has always allowed her mother to do that. She has always been so obedient.

Kitty tells Caroline about her job. Caroline fully understands that Kitty does not like her job. Kitty explains that she wants to do something else, but does not know what she really wants and that she received an offer from a career coach to go to Scotland and find out what she really likes. Caroline thinks this a fantastic idea and wants to go with her! After some back and forth, they decide to go together. Kitty is not sure if this is really a good idea as Caroline always dominates her environment. Will she do what Caroline wants? She thinks it is all rather scary and worries about how to tell her boss at work.

Eventually she decides to go with Caroline and is relieved when there are no objections at work. When she calls her mother to tell her that she is going to Scotland with Caroline, her mother says: "With Caroline? Well, if you think this is good for you, go ahead and do it. But I worry a bit..." In the background she hears her father say: "Good, she can bring me a bottle of Scotch."

Adventures in Scotland

After arriving in Findhorn, Scotland, it takes Kitty a few days before she begins to enjoy herself. She feels very closely connected to the group and does all kinds of things she never thought she would enjoy. Luckily, Caroline is in another group and returns home after a week. But Kitty adds another week. With six other participants, she plants trees in the Scottish Highlands together with a Scottish couple she meets, John and Linda. Kitty finds their ideas a little vague, but she is fascinated by the rough outdoors life. She says that for the first time in her life she feels really alive. She can feel her muscles, and her arms are covered with scratches and mosquito bites, which makes her feel very proud. She also has a 'real' boyfriend. It is all very exciting!

Her parents worry about what Kitty is doing, but she just 'forgets' to call them. She sends an occasional text message that she is all right. Kitty's musical talents are greatly appreciated. In the evening there is often singing around the campfire and people are impressed with her voice. She has not brought her violin, as it is too fragile. Besides, her fingers are stiff from the rough work, so she wouldn't have been able to play anyway.

She decides to stay for another month and resigns from her position as a PhD student. Her parents are very disappointed and think that that is foolish. But Kitty really enjoys the interesting contacts and her rough wildlife experience. However, she also realizes that planting trees and becoming a forest ranger is not her final destination (her mother does not need to worry, however, she does not tell her.)

Longing to see her girlfriends, she goes home for a weekend. Although her parents are still very critical of her choice (despite the beautiful pictures of Scotland, she has taken), they notice her radiance. "We have not seen you like this for a long time!" they say. Kitty decides to sign on for one more month and then she will return to the Netherlands, her native country. She has no idea what she will do next, but she is fully confident that she will find something that will suit her. She now knows what real living is. And she has become much more assertive. She has also experienced how it feels to make your own choices. She would not have missed this adventure for the world!

Motivation
Kitty notices in Scotland that she has no desire at all to work as a PhD student. She realizes that she has taken this position mainly to please her parents. Her brother Bob, with whom she still has a very good relationship, wanted to become a writer, went against his parents' wishes, and has already published a couple of short stories.

Kitty now knows what she does *not* want, but she doesn't really know what she *does* want. She notices that she still is inclined to accommodate people and do what others want her to do. She also sees that this does not make her happy. She knows that she has to stay away from her parents and find her own way.

How to proceed?
Based on what Kitty experienced in Scotland, she wants to do the following:

Change her contact with her parents
Up to this time, Kitty too often did what she thought her parents wanted. Although she really likes her parents, this now bothers her. She wants to make her own choices and decides to sit down with her parents and tell them that. She trains for that talk with a girlfriend who gives her tips.
In addition, she decides to start looking for her own apartment as soon as possible and move out.

Working on her career choice
She resigns her PhD Studentship position and her supervisor tells her she thinks that is a mistake. But Kitty does not want to go back or chose another, similar job. For a while she just wants to make money somewhere as a waitress while thinking about her next steps. She is still young, so she has plenty of time to look. Besides, she can always switch jobs!

Kitty really enjoyed her singing experience in Scotland. She signs up for singing lessons and a theater orientation course. This course trains students to become drama therapists. This is one of the options that appeal to her. But she also thinks about studying music. She loves folk music and also considers learning to play the guitar, so she can accompany herself. Or maybe she can work on something to do with the environment.

Private
The boyfriend in Scotland is long gone. She was sad about that, but she realizes that keeping in touch was not an option. She starts going out a little more frequently hoping to meet suitable men. It has become much easier for her to make contacts.

To recap
We discuss Kitty's story in our peer group discussion. Below is a short report about our conversation.

The occupational physician
Kitty is now working hard to find out what work would suit her and what would be a good working environment. I have treated quite a few gifted people who experience stress when they turn forty and realize they have made the wrong career decision and have been working for years in situations that do not fit their capabilities and talents. These are often people who depend too much on their reasoning and too little on their feelings. When you are over forty, change is much harder (but not impossible, of course). I am confident that Kitty will make it! Do you recognize that, in yourself too?

The psychologist/coach
Kitty is gifted but apparently had trouble breaking away from her parents, especially her mother. She finds it hard to choose because she has so many talents. She is very smart, musical and social and has many girlfriends. In high school she was challenged when choosing subjects. That happened again when it came time to choose her field of study and when looking for a suitable job. It appears that she let her parents, with whom she has a good relationship, guide her in her choices.

Kitty adapted to her environment, and seemed to adapt to the expectations of people who are important to her. Because of that, she ignored her own desires and she no longer knew what she really wanted. The results of her behavior are already noticeable when she is 23. She still lived with her parents and was uncertain about her own choices.

Only when she finally starts with the outdoor adventures does she discover what she enjoys. Suddenly, all kinds of talents appear. Kitty, it turns out, is adventurous, daring, deals well with situations where the results aren't certain and is curious about what life will bring.

She bought time by taking a job. Apparently she now has enough self-confidence and assumes that in time something will come her way – something that she will commit to because *she* likes it. That demands courage, which she has developed. But I believe that this is only the beginning of her road to independence and making choices based on what she wants for *herself.* Her giftedness and insight into how this had worked for her so far, will help her make good choices the next time she feels uncertain again.

6. I know better....

**When Edward Browning, 30, completed his internship
following medical school, he knew that he did not want to
continue his career in a hospital because the atmosphere
there did not appeal to him. Physicians did not have enough
time with their patients. And in discussions with special-
ists he noticed that other critical thinkers like him were not
really accepted. Edward especially disliked the rigid hier-
archy, the pecking order.**

He decided to become a school doctor[4] and joined a department of school health that covered schools in nine towns in
the middle of the Netherlands. Within a year, Edward was
bored. He had thought of many ways to make the work more
interesting and meaningful, but he was unsuccessful in
persuading the head of the group to support his proposals,
as she believed that the towns' financial system did not
permit any flexibility.

His next career step was to search for a position in England,
also in social medicine, but Edward found out most opportunities required him to first have worked in a British hospital,
which he did not want to do. Then he saw an advert for a position as an occupational physician in the Netherlands that
looked interesting. He secured the position and immersed
himself in the work, expecting that the most important parts
of his work would be in preventive medicine.

Now he is finding in practice, that he spends most of his time
providing guidance to employees who are out on medical leave.
Though disappointed, he tries to perform his job well, but
observes that systems and procedures are lax. For example,

---

4   A school doctor in the Netherlands is a specialist in social medicine, who advises stu-
     dents, parents and schools regarding medical matters.

he quickly notices that most of his colleagues fail to complete a good medical history or perform a proper physical examination. How can you analyze or deliver responsible advices without obtaining a history first? Edward has a strong opinion on this point and knows that numerous medical articles support his view. He also believes that the context of the patient's life, such as problems at home, should be taken into account in a physician's assessment.

Edward starts a discussion with his colleagues at work, but they look at him in surprise, wondering what he means. He tries again in a meeting with colleagues. He suggests that their process could be improved by following scientific insights and the evidence based guidelines formulated by the professional organizations. He also proposes that physicians are morally required to take into account the employee's circumstances, e.g. his or her private life, when giving advice. As a health and safety organization, he says that they should emphasize the benefits of health care and safety in order to convince employers to adopt them.

Edward wants to do scientific research and work with a university and is fairly forceful in the arguments he puts forward. He gets increasingly upset during the discussion, and becomes louder and louder, ignoring his colleagues' arguments. His colleagues and supervisor feel that he is a bully and a know-it-all and reject his ideas. Edward is very disappointed to no longer be appreciated for, or get satisfaction from, his work. He wants to break out of the deadlock, but does not know who can help him.

During an evaluation his supervisor, Chris, says to Edward: "I think your goals are fine, but the way you present them is not, as it creates a lot of resistance amongst your colleagues. You are too obsessive and you do not listen to anyone else's arguments. And there is a lot of criticism about the way you work. I hear, you sometimes have your patients wait for an hour because all of a sudden you think of something else interesting. And you often start your office hours late. What about your planning?" Edward explodes, shouting he has never seen such a bunch of idiots.

Chris finds Edward's behavior unacceptable and asks him to take medical leave and to visit the occupational health physician who works for their own staff. Edward does not even contemplate doing that. Why should he visit a colleague occupational physician who does not even keep up with his own profession? If there is something wrong with him, he is certain he would know it himself.

Chris is at a loss as to how to deal with the situation and anonymously asks a Work and Organizational psychologist in his own network for advice. This psychologist advises that Edward should talk to a colleague of his through the health and safety service, who has a contract to help employees. When Chris suggests this idea to Edward, he initially resists. Only when Edward's wife also says that she finds him aggressive, unreasonable and does not want to stay with him, does he reluctantly decide to talk to the psychologist.

Analysis of the situation
This is what the psychologist reports from the consultation she had with Edward:

As is the case with many gifted people Edward has already had several types of jobs at a fairly young age but does not feel at home anywhere. He demands a lot from his work and has a high moral standard, expecting the same from his colleagues as he does from himself. However, his high expectations are rarely met. His colleagues find him to be an obsessive know-it-all. His supervisor thinks he should cut back on his work a bit. Edward has become ever more frustrated and tense and that does not help his relationship with his colleagues. Tension with his wife is also increasing. Edward thinks he cannot break out of this pattern. He does not understand that working successfully requires other skills than just his medical expertise.

Reflection on the situation
The Work and Organizational psychologist reports the following about her conversation with Edward.

Dealing with obstructing thoughts
Edward explains his view of the situation, talking a lot and doesn't hear me when I occasionally ask a question or make a remark. During the conversation Edward becomes increasingly angry about the problems he has with his colleagues and his work. He is only able to think at one level – the cognitive level. He also tries to convince me that he is right, as far as logic is concerned. His reasoning is watertight. There is nothing wrong with his arguments, but I notice he criticizes others a lot and has little insight into the effects of his own behavior on others. I hold a mirror up to him, but Edward does not look into it.

Dealing with emotions
During the conversation Edward becomes increasingly excited, sometimes banging his fist on the table and yelling that I also refuse to understand him. I tell him that I find his reactions a bit excessive and ask why he is so upset. Initially he denies that he is angry. He says the fact that nobody understands him, not even his wife, makes him desperate. He is afraid he will lose his wife. Edward feels as if no one understands him and feels incapable of explaining what he thinks is important and why. This very conversation is yet another experience and disappointment among many and that makes him very angry.

Edward calms down when he understands that this situation has been going on for a long time and that it started early in his life. His being gifted (which he had found out recently) gives him insights that others do not share with him. Understanding this also makes him sad.

We continue this discussion during the next meeting. It is hard for Edward to grasp that he may be right, but that no one will agree with him because of his behavior.

He cannot grasp how to switch to the relationship level *(see chapter 4)*, so I ask him to read a number of books about this subject so that he will gain more insight into his own behavior. I ask him to identify similar experiences in his past. At the next meeting he says that he found that painful, so he didn't do it, because, he says, "he didn't have time for it."

His great anger strikes me, as well as his fear of dealing with it. I try to understand what Edward means using pictures and metaphors, in other words: indirectly. I tell him a story about an inventor and a princess. The inventor only has eyes for his inventions, lives by himself and suddenly a princess, who is lost, visits him.
What should the inventor do? When he starts liking her more and more, how can he tell her? Edward reacts in a very distant way. Actually he does nothing until I, playing the princess, let him know that I rather like him. Edward feels very uncomfortable about this. It is too close to home, he says, and this scares him. He hides his fears by using verbal aggression. I propose that he discuss the theme of intimacy with a clinical psychologist and that his wife might want to participate in those conversations also.

During the next session we play the game 'The king and the servant,' where the servant serves the king. Edward is the servant. In this game Edward recognizes his relationship with his father who always tried to outdo him and found it hard to accept that Edward was much smarter than him. Edward had to hold back his anger frequently, but at the same time he was very upset that he was being belittled. Edward's father was in the military and had little patience with him. Fortunately, Edward understood things very quickly and knew exactly what he had to do so that he would not become the target of his father's anger.
Actually he did this more and more often, Edward says, adjusting to a situation where he didn't feel happy, or simply leaving, became his way of life.

He realizes that this is the first time he has shared his true thoughts with another person, but not in a very effective way, he thinks.

I also start using transactional analysis *(see text box)* with Edward because I recognize much of the Controlling (or Critical) Parent in his behavior. When Edward begins to see the effects of his behavior from the viewpoint of a Critical Parent position, he will gain better insight into his own attitude and behavior.

Because he chooses to act as a critical parent, his colleagues react from the Child Position, which does not lead to constructive conversations. With this insight, which he rather likes, Edward can begin to explore other approaches (the Adult Position and the Nurturing Parent). Based on these views he begins to ask for his colleagues' thoughts, input and opinions, offers constructive feedback, and shows an interest in the objections and/or questions his colleagues have.

In other words: Edward starts listening better and commits to what the other person wants to say, both nonverbally and verbally, without immediately wanting to be right. This new behavior will demand a lot of patience from him, but once he learns not only to look at the content, but also at the communication process (not *what* he says, but *how* he says it) he may be able to use his knowledge and skills to come up with win – win scenarios.

Transactional analysis and ego positions
People can think, feel and act in different ways. Sometimes they will be excited, sometimes depressed, sometimes bossy, sometimes concerned, sometimes sober and businesslike, then like a headless chicken. People can be in different states. Transactional Analysis (T.A.) calls these states I–positions or ego-positions.
There are three different groups of ego positions: the Parent Position, the Adult Position and the Child

Position. These three parts form the structure of our personality. We are in one of these three ego positions every moment of the day. We can change ego positions and that is why we act as a child at one moment and as a parent or adult at another moment.

Parent Position
This is the ego position in which the individual feels, thinks and acts like his or her parent(s).
This ego position is subdivided into:
a. The Controlling (or Critical) Parent: the parent who sets standards and limitations.
b. The Nurturing Parent: the parent who is nurturing and protects.

Adult Position
The Adult is the ego position that collects and investigates information. This information is stored and used to calculate probabilities. It is directed at the reality of the now.

Child Position
This is the structured whole of all behavior, feelings and convictions based on the individual's own history.
This ego position is subdivided into:
a. The Free Child: spontaneous, creative (positive) and immature (negative).
b. The Adapted Child: accommodating to the outside world: Co-operative (positive) and Compliant/ Resistant (negative).

All people may act based on these three ego positions. Adults don't just have the Adult Position available; they also have the Parent and Child options. Children can also behave based on their Adult or their Parent Position. It is desirable that there is a balance among Parent, Adult and Child Positions; otherwise there will be negative consequences.
(See for more information: Stewart & Jones, 2012.)

Many conversations later, some of Edward's aggressive behavior has disappeared and he is more open to learning how to have a conversation and how to switch to different levels (content and relationship level, nonverbal and verbal signals in communication). This happens after we had a lively discussion of Watzlawick's theory *(see chapter 4)* – where I can't fault his reasoning and soon am unable to get in a word edgeways. Edward comes to understand his anger and the way he wants to be proven right. He also becomes more relaxed at home, although he still has a long way to go in his relationship with his wife.

Motivation
Edward grows to realize that his being gifted causes him to achieve the opposite of what he wants. Although he has reflected on his work environment earlier, he now once again reviews what motivates him professionally. He finds he is driven to apply scientific insights in his work. This includes his great commitment to the clients and also to the organization (which had been almost invisible because of all the clashes). He really wants to contribute to a better image of the Health and Safety Service. Edward sees many opportunities in his current job, although he needs space to also perform (scientific) research and explore new treatment methods. Edward realizes that if he learns to communicate in a more open way and to connect with the questions his colleagues want answered, he can gain a lot for himself, meaning he can better show what he can do.

Reflection on the situation
Through our conversations Edward learns that the way he has worked until now creates a great deal of resistance. He also gains more insight into the reasons behind his behavior. This insight gives him much peace of mind. He realizes that there are other ways by which he can approach things. If he can present his point-of-view in a more tactful way and if he can take into account his colleagues' arguments (even if he does not think much of them) the organization may pursue Edward's

interests in new developments. He can make money for the organization through his scientific insights. Demand for scientific support for treatment and guidance methods is increasing, and Edward enjoys writing about that. This would mean that Edward's supervisor will need to give him more space and to inform the other employees of the situation, who may otherwise quickly feel 'insulted' by Edward.

How to proceed?
Together we discuss a number of possible options for Edward.

Conversation with his supervisor
Edward discusses with Chris the need for more scientific research. He also asks Chris for support in case he observes that Edward is focusing so much on his idea that he creates resistance among his colleagues. Chris reacts positively and is happy that Edward is reacting in a more collegial way and with less frustration. It is an enormous victory for Edward when he wins Chris over, and he regains the motivation he needs to do his job.

Learning to communicate
Edward wants to learn about his communication patterns. How can he become more effective in dealing with resistance and learn how to persuade others to join him? He finds a book in the library about working together. This publication provides many practical suggestions for communicating with 'difficult' people.
Maybe Edward might also find it useful to help with his behavior towards clients and in his private life.

By learning to negotiate, Edward can experience the results of cooperation and competition with his colleagues. Before, when he felt that he was not 'winning', Edward behaved in a way that was more obsessive, as a 'know-it-all'. In such circumstances communication broke down because Edward behaved as if his colleagues were useless nitwits ("Now listen well this time because who amongst us knows anything about evidence-based treatment methods? Me, of course.") His colleagues' reactions would probably be: "Sure, Edward, of course, but not just now." Or they would ask for a copy of his idea and throw it away immediately.

In any case, they did nothing with Edward's ideas. So this pattern has to be broken. Edward can do this by saying: "Gee, I notice that you don't like my ideas. What do you think would be a good method? Maybe we can exchange a few ideas?" Or his colleague might say: "Edward, it may be a great idea, but I don't have time to discuss it with you right now. Let's discuss it another time, or organize a meeting. Then I can share my thoughts on your proposal." In terms of working together, this example describes a shift from competitive to consultative exchanges of ideas. Instead of arguing with each other, they listen to each other's arguments, give feedback and start a discussion about the subject. This is how to create a win-win situation for everyone and shows how people can learn from each other.

Talking with the University

Edward wants to explore whether he can channel his passion as a guest lecturer at the University into something positive. Maybe he can do more with his interest in theory and in supporting treatment methods in this environment.

Looking for help for his relationship with his wife

Edward worries about his relationship with his wife. He wants to stay with his wife, but in the last few years has felt increasingly powerless.

He believes that his wife does not understand him. Only after our discussions does he develop insight into the causes and effects of his aggressive attitude. His wife has wanted to seek help earlier, but at that point Edward did not see the use. But he also did not feel able to solve the problems by himself. So he (reluctantly) agrees with his wife's proposal to look for help with their relationship.

To recap

The Work and Organizational psychologist discusses her experiences with Edward with an occupational physician in her peer group discussion. Here is what she reports:

Edward's expectations of his job were (too) high. He didn't understand the fact that being a gifted person made him different, even in an academic environment. Also, his communication difficulties made it hard for him to clarify what he found to be important in his work. Both of these issues contributed to his colleagues' inability to understand him, to which Edward reacted with unacceptable emotional outbursts. He lost his balance and fell into a sinkhole. Increasingly he acted more arrogantly towards his colleagues and his supervisor, lecturing them and ignoring the importance of self-reflection. He became increasingly dogmatic in his views regarding theoretical foundations and no longer saw that there were other ways to think about the issues. As for emotions, I was struck by his high level of aggressiveness. It was hard to make progress because of a lot of old injuries. His complaints 'I feel misunderstood,' came up frequently. And his fear of intimacy was a factor. I think this is something for a therapist to work on.

My approach was focused on increasing his understanding of the causes and effects of his behavior towards his own environment. Edward has started to communicate differently. He also benefits from having to think more deeply about his own motivations. I believe his current job can offer him what he needs, to a certain extent, but it is advisable that he speaks with someone at the University. Who knows, there may be an opportunity for Edward to pursue a PhD? And he should continue working with his wife on their relationship. We will not discuss that here, but improving his relationship would probably also benefit his work.

7. Pain everywhere, what now?

Frances Williams, 35, works part-time as a secretary in a medium-sized real estate office. She started university at 17, studying math and anthropology, but dropped out, thinking there was no point in studying these subjects. After working as a temporary secretary for a time, she joined the real estate firm almost five years ago and does some freelance PR and editorial work as well. Most PR work at the real estate firm is outsourced, which she doesn't like because she has ideas she would like to contribute.

Frances is very involved in her work. She is the office's first point of contact with customers and she has devised a contact system to register and monitor customer telephone calls, agreements, and activities, to make it easier for everybody in her office to work with customers.
The system enables employees to keep tabs on everyone's activities. The system works so well that sales has increased significantly. Her colleagues think the system is a wonderful innovation, but Frances herself doesn't think it is anything special.

Last year Frances started to feel pain in her neck and shoulders. More recently, she developed pain in her arms and wrists. She believes that these problems are caused by her heavy use of the computer. To deal with the pain she took sick days, and recently spent two weeks at home.

She discusses her medical issues with her supervisor, the director of the real estate office, and suggests her work-space be modified to prevent her pain. The office recently did something similar for a girlfriend. Frances asks for an adjustable desk, a better chair, a wrist support, new keyboard, break software. Her supervisor responds that an official health and safety inspection has recently reviewed and approved all workspaces. He tells Frances that her requests are too much; having heard from colleagues that such equipment is expensive and often ends up in storage spaces, unused. Moreover, he has already invested in changes in the workspaces. As for Frances's complaints, he believes her issues are not only job-related. He is fed up with all her 'problems' regarding workspaces. He values Frances' work, because she always understands exactly what he wants, writes perfect letters, is very customer-friendly and works very well with her colleagues. But Frances' frequently being absent because she feels sick causes problems in his office. Response to customers' questions is much slower and not as good and sales are suffering. When Frances complains about loud conversations in the office and about the radio being turned on occasionally, he proposes she talks to the occupational physician. Frances completely disagrees, believing she is treated unfairly.

Given the major contributions she has made to the office's sales, she is upset that her supervisor will not invest in her workspace. Frances believes her supervisor is required to provide a good work environment. So she becomes sullen, especially as she investigates and finds that an adapted work space will not cost all that much. She complains to her colleagues about her supervisor and increasingly avoids contact with him. Because of her pain she has less energy and time for her friends and her hobbies.
Frances loves music and at one time enjoyed singing and playing the cello, but is no longer able to do either because of the pain. She also lacks the energy to visit her family and friends, leaving her frequently home alone. Frances visits her general physician, but decides he does not know any-thing. So she checks out the Internet herself to see what her problems might be. When Frances again calls in sick, her supervisor wants her to visit the occupational physician to talk to her about her complaints and their possible con-nection to her workspace.

Even though Frances absolutely disagrees with her supervisor, she decides to make an appointment with the occupational physician. Frances hopes the doctor will be more reasonable than her supervisor....

Analysis of the situation

Frances is probably a gifted woman. She started two university studies, but didn't finish them. She didn't see the point and started working as a secretary. She does her work very well and is an asset to the office, for example, by designing the new customer service system. She herself did not think it was anything special, but the people around her did. In addition she is overly sensitive to sound. She researches all kind of information by herself about her different physical complaints. Frances enjoys various hobbies in addition to her work and is very focused on them. These are some of the characteristics that point to the likelihood that Frances is gifted. She calls in sick with complaints about pain in her arms and shoulders and bad headaches. Frances is rather compulsive about her pain complaints, which have affected her social life which she likes very much. Frances is really at the end of her rope. Despite the steps she has taken, the pain persists. So what now? As mentioned before, she goes to the occupational physician.

Reflection on the situation

Frances meets several times with the occupational physician, telling her that the pain in her shoulders and wrists has increased over the last year after she started performing more repetitive tasks. The office has also become busier, so that she no longer has time to do the things she likes better. Her manager now outsources those kinds of jobs and her work is focused exclusively on the computer. She does not enjoy that type of routine work and is also very angry with her supervisor because he does not want to invest in her workspace. She claims that her colleagues greatly value her.

The occupational physician explains:

Dealing with obstructive thoughts
When I question her about her complaints, Frances says
that she has experienced headaches since she was very
young and has read a great deal about the topic. Based on
her research, she had all of her amalgam fillings in her teeth
replaced in an effort to get rid of her headaches. She also
had her whole apartment checked for magnetic and electri-
cal radiation. And she maintains a strict diet. "Sometimes it
takes over my whole life, yes, and eating out is almost
impossible with my diet. Such a diet is also very hard to
maintain during vacations and trips...," she says. I notice
that Frances researched many facts, but focused on external factors, hardly noticing that the way she deals with her
complaints might also influence her pain.
When I broach the subject, Frances is not open to that idea.
When I propose she talk with a psychologist and do some
relaxation exercises with the aid of a physiotherapist, Frances initially becomes very angry. "I am just asking for some
adjustments at work." I explain that blaming everything on
your environment, also called 'external locus of control,'
means you have no control of your own situation. Frances
thinks about that for a while and eventually she agrees
(although with reluctance) to talk to a psychologist. She
changed her mind because she is still experiencing considerable pain and she wants to get rid of that because she
wants to go back to (part-time) work.

Frances visits a psychologist.
In her conversation with the psychologist, Frances explains
that her social life has suffered greatly because of her complaints. She used to be in frequent contact with her sister
and enjoyed playing games with her cousins, who are very
intelligent. But she is in too much pain to do that now.
Below is the report by the psychologist.

The psychologist
I ask Frances when she first noticed her symptoms emerging. She says that she has had headaches for many years. Often the headaches would appear unexpectedly, but sometimes she could feel them coming on but if she took medication in time, she was able to work.
The complaints in her neck, shoulders and wrists started a year ago. In Frances' view, the issues are caused by her heavy use of the computer. She has no time to do other things once in a while.

I tell Frances that I am concerned about her. Despite her complaints, she is still *demanding* so much from herself.
I also notice the almost compulsive way in which she maintains her diet. I ask if she ever *allows* herself to do something, instead of *having to do* so much. What would happen if she just leaves her computer? Or, if she follows a less strict diet? What disaster would happen?
It is hard to convince Frances to look at her complaints in a different way. It takes time before she realizes there may be other solutions than adjusting her workspace. When I ask her to write down alternative solutions, however crazy, I am surprised that she comes back with an appreciable list.
She wants to join one of her colleagues looking at a house with a client or visiting an open house once in a while.
And she wants to create a beautiful website for the office.
And she also wants to become an opera singer. She has so many ambitions! She dreams of being able to eat at a top restaurant once a week! Her list offers a number of points for me to hold follow-up conversations with her about her job, her life, what inspires her. Meanwhile, she is still in a great deal of pain and considers going to the physiotherapist to lower the tension in her body.

When she finally goes, it brings up many emotions. Frances is still very angry with her supervisor, thinking of herself as the 'victim.' But Frances also feels her own loneliness. She is also far from pleased about herself and her work, a realization that she fears to confront.

Dealing with emotions

During the next conversation I ask Frances about critical choices she made in her life and how she felt about them at the time. Frances can describe the turning points, but finds it hard to describe her feelings. For example, I ask her about dropping out of college. Frances replies that she "couldn't see the point of it", but when I probe deeper she says that the material didn't answer her questions and the stupidity of her fellow students bothered her. She had not said anything about that before! Eventually she stopped studying and 'simply' started working. "And because I couldn't do anything, I decided to just work here as a secretary. But I am really bored, I am unhappy and I hate that routine work."

During these conversations I notice that Frances is often angry, at other people, but also at herself. But she only notices her anger much later. And she finds it 'scary.' She really hates conflict. She doesn't know how to deal with her feelings, because she fears that if she reveals them, nobody will like her anymore. She does notice that she often develops headaches when she represses her feelings in a situation of conflict. We role-play a number of conflict situations. I play her supervisor and observe that Frances reacts as if she has been wronged and expects her supervisor to let her do what she wants without telling him exactly what she wants, I call that 'waiting for Santa Claus': not making a wish list and expecting Santa to guess what you want, and then being angry when you receive a computer game instead of an electric car. Frances recognizes this, so we start a wish list, first for her workspace, then for her work and finally for her life.

I ask her to write a story about her dream job. I can see that Frances is uncomfortable, but she does not say anything. When she comes back with two lines, I ask why she has not written a full story. First she evades answering, but then she says she thought it was a stupid assignment. I ask her to suggest a better assignment. Frances has thought about her dream job and just wants to talk about it based on a book she read. She is very enthusiastic about doing something in public relations. She has already done some public relations work when she was a student, and says she was very good at it.

I go back to our conversation. Initially Frances didn't say that she didn't feel like doing the assignment and only did part of it. But we don't fight about it. Realizing that you don't have to fight if you don't want to do something is liberating for Frances.

Frances discusses her wish list with her supervisor. She indicates she would like to do less routine work and asks if she may do the PR work, which would save her supervisor a lot of money. When her supervisor reacts positively, Frances' pain situation improves. She becomes more aware of her emotions also, thanks to her physiotherapy. We continue working on that. What is she feeling and what does she do with those feelings? We also discuss her loneliness, which dates back to her early life. Frances was bullied as a child and cried a lot. This also made her vulnerable, so she started 'swallowing her tears.' Only halfway through high school did she get friends and girlfriends, which made her quite happy. Then, she 'did everything' to keep them. She now understands that the way she reacted came at the expense of her own desires.

Six months later (when she had already returned to working full-time) Frances understands much better what she really wants and is more aware of her feelings, although she still finds it hard to express them. We role-play every 'difficult' situation so that she can maintain 'control of her feelings' as she puts it.

Motivation
Frances explains that her current work is below her level. Through the discussions about her job, she is able to get more in touch with what really drives her in her work. Frances starts thinking more about herself and her plans for the future.

She realizes that she let most fun jobs at her work, namely the PR work, the ads and the leaflets, pass by and has not let her supervisor know that she could do those jobs, too. Even more importantly, she has not let him know that she is good at those tasks and also enjoys them very much. Frances has great creative abilities, including drawing and writing. She discovers how important it is for her to have a good atmosphere at work. She has agreeable colleagues and feels valued. She wants to know more about real estate. Maybe she can take a course ... All of a sudden Frances finds so many enjoyable things to do that she doesn't know what to choose. Eventually she decides to focus on PR and advertising for the real estate office.

How to proceed?
During the counseling process Frances herself chooses the following actions.

A talk with her supervisor
Frances overcomes her natural shyness and together with the psychologist sets up a plan describing what she wants in her work and her workspace. She submits it to her supervisor and he agrees to test adjusting her workspace. That is a success! Frances also wants to be more involved in helping clients find places to live. Her supervisor agrees that she will be good working with single women. This is a part of the business that is not doing very well. However, he knows he will then need a part-time secretary to cover the routine tasks that Frances has been doing.

Her supervisor immediately agrees that Frances take on advertising and PR work, having noticed her talents and realizing that she could save him money. He wants to keep Frances because he considers her a good employee! Frances is very enthusiastic about all the opportunities that have opened up for her and notices that the pain in her shoulders and wrists is bothering her much less.

Relaxation
Frances starts looking for relaxing activities to do in her spare time. She loves music but the pain in her shoulders currently makes it impossible for her to play the cello, so she looks for a choir. She also considers taking singing lessons. She is especially interested in South American folk music. Through the singing lessons she learns how to relax her body. In addition, she joins a girlfriend in going to a gym. Exercising with the fitness equipment is hard, but after a few weeks she notices the pain in her arms has decreased. That motivates her to continue.

To recap
The occupational physician and the psychologist discuss their experiences with Frances.

The occupational physician
Frances came to my office with what she called RSI complaints. Currently we prefer to call this 'CANS.' *(See also the information chapter.)*

Frances thought making technical adjustments to her workspace might solve her complaints. I believed that technical equipment would not help her for the long term, because we have learned that these kinds of complaints are mainly caused by the way people work, building tension in their neck and shoulders. Such problems are often observed in perfectionist and conscientious employees. You don't solve these kinds of problems with just technology. That is why I initially explained to Frances that her way of dealing with complaints was linked to where she put her 'locus of control.' Below I note what I told her and why 'locus of control' is often linked to chronic pain.

Locus of control
Some people naturally place the cause of their complaints outside of themselves and as a result also place the possible solutions there. We call that an external 'locus of control.'

Chronic pain
People with unexplainable chronic pain often place the cause of that pain outside of themselves. They are a major problem for many physicians, as these patients put their problems into the doctor's hands. Often no medical issues are found. But these patients have real complaints, so the solution is to help them heal themselves, e.g. with the aid of a psychologist, coach or counselor. If the complaints are long-standing, a multidisciplinary approach, e.g. the combination of physiotherapy and psychology, often appears effective.

I very quickly recognized Frances to be a gifted woman. There were a number of indicators, including the fact she didn't finish her studies and the way in which she collected information for herself. In cases of very intelligent people I often notice that they are very much aware of their physical pain, which is often a signal of overload or insufficient relaxation. However, these persons are often unable to deal with these complaints. Frances, too, ignored her problems and worked way too long. She even started working harder. But suddenly she couldn't go on.
In her situation she caught it just in time, but sometimes this can lead to nervous exhaustion and burnout and in that case it often takes a very long time before a person can overcome these problems *(see also chapter 2 and the information chapter)*. When I heard her story about her complaints about headaches during her childhood, I thought there was a parallel between her current complaints and the way she was dealing with them.

The psychologist

I recognized many characteristics of being gifted while listening to her complaints and her way of analyzing them. Her job was certainly below her capacities. When her work became ever more routine, Frances developed ever more complaints. When she wasn't able to resolve the situation with her supervisor, she called in sick. Because of her past experiences, Frances had not learned how to express her own desires; she was afraid of conflicts and suppressed her own anger and sadness. Eventually, she almost got stuck. When she had no energy to see her sister and her friends, she had reached the end of her tether. She had lost her bearings, which finally forced her to do something about her situation. Fortunately, she did trust her occupational physician so that she could take the first steps.

As I spoke with Frances, I noticed that she had many talents but took only limited responsibility for her situation. She felt she was a victim.
She knew exactly what was happening regarding her complaints and what the solution was. When I heard all the things she had researched in the alternative circuit, I agreed with the occupational physician. Frances looked too much outside herself and didn't pay enough attention to the way she dealt with her complaints. During our conversations we worked a lot on this. At the same time I thought her proposal to her supervisor to adjust her workspace using a number of cheap resources was definitely reasonable. Only that would not solve the problem for the long-term, because there was always a chance that Frances would develop other complaints if she didn't start addressing her working too hard and her own motives in her work.
Doing this would enable her to set her own course and control her own life. I was able to go through her difficult situations step-by-step and make her experience the things that can make life difficult. For example, her own intrusive thoughts were an issue: 'I must be liked,' or 'I am powerless.' Sometimes I joked about that or I had her describe the possible disasters.

That taught her to put things into a better perspective. We also laughed a lot together. In addition, we addressed choices she had made in her private life.

By recognizing her problems and using her very own way of approaching them, Frances eventually came up with her own solutions and she executed them herself. Her supervisor gave her a chance to do other work that fit her much better.

8. My way or the highway

Bastian Schaefer, age 53, owns a small woodworking company where he builds furniture and designs very unique pieces. He has a sense of humor, but Bastian becomes extremely angry when things do not work out the way that he would like. He lashes out at everything and everyone, especially his wife and children.

Bastian was the youngest of five children, the only son. His family lived in the eastern part of the country, where his father was a thoracic surgeon and his mother a volunteer who worked with the handicapped. When Bastian was born, his mother was ecstatic. A son, finally! Suddenly she paid much less attention to her daughters. Bastian was her favorite. His sisters, who spent a good deal of time together, took every chance to bully him, especially when Bastian became angry. His mother tried to protect him, but of course she didn't see and hear everything. Bastian was an enterprising and visibly intelligent child. When he was in grade school, he regularly went exploring, trying to find out how the world works. For example, one beautiful summer afternoon, he just walked out of school with two friends to go chase rabbits together.
When the boys didn't return, the police were called. Bastian was very surprised. If he felt like chasing rabbits, why should he sit in school where he didn't learn anything? Bastian was very interested in other animals, too. He caught frogs' eggs, put them in an aquarium and studied the various stages of the frogs' development. Sometimes he killed one and dissected it very carefully.

Bastian also found cars very exciting, especially how their mechanics worked. Sometimes he went to the scrap yard, collected all the usable parts he could find and used them to build something completely new.

Bastian was very conceited. Since he was right, he certainly would not listen to his mother and his sisters. He didn't have much contact with his sisters anyway. Bastian spent a lot of time in his room where he worked on his own hobbies, such as taking apart radios, putting them together again, and working on a large car racetrack.

Bastian easily completed high school and, at age 17, moved out of his parents' house and enrolled in college to study economics. Bastian enjoyed the student life and that was the reason it took him seven years to finish. He really didn't enjoy economics, but he did want to make a lot of money so that he could buy the beautiful cars he liked.

After his studies, Bastian quickly found a position with a large bank but resisted following the rules. As long as he did his work well, he decided, it didn't matter if he was late; when that happened, he just worked later. And he decided it was not necessary to wear a tie. Customers should just trust his word; it didn't matter what he looked like. Bastian did not remain quiet if he disagreed with something. Although he did his work very well, he ran into problems. For that reason, Bastian decided to start his own company, so that he could do whatever he wanted.

In the meantime he had found a girlfriend, Maria. He bought a small house in the countryside and renovated it together with Maria. When she became pregnant, they married and started their own company. Bastian worked day and night. He knew a lot about wood and which type of wood worked best for a particular project. He also thoroughly enjoyed designing furniture and making wood sculptures, which were very original and creative. He advertised his knowledge and skills very well and his customers valued his abilities.

However, for quite some time things have not been going very well. For instance problems often pop up when the pieces have to be delivered to customers.

Not only does Bastian hardly ever meet the deadline, he also does not do a very good job with his company's administration. Sometimes it isn't clear where the furniture must be delivered; costs aren't broken out, etc. Usually, Bastian then becomes very angry and blames Maria, who can't cope with this verbal violence. She tries to soothe him, but that makes Bastian even more angry. Eventually Maria manages deliveries by herself as much as possible. Bastian tends to treat her as his servant.

Over the years they had two boys and two girls and moved to a large house in the country, where Bastian created a company office at home. He works all day and that leads to major tensions in his family. Bastian doesn't like his daughters because they do not exhibit much respect for authority. If they don't do what he tells them, Bastian hits them.
Bastian has purchased several fine cars with his profits, giving each son their own car. Bastian drives at least 110 miles an hour on the highway when he has a chance. He ignores every traffic ticket. He thinks, "Why would you turn right at a roundabout if you can also turn left?" After all, that is safe because there is no traffic at that time. He thinks the traffic ticket he receives for that incident is absolute nonsense. Even when it snows and the road is slippery, Bastian thinks that he can still drive 60 miles an hour on the left side of the road, even if his wife is terrified. In his own mind, Bastian believes that he has his car completely under control, and, surprisingly, he has very few accidents.

At home, tension continues to increase because his children don't tolerate his authoritarian behavior. Last month Bastian started experiencing chest pains. He also feels tired and listless. After a new burst of anger, Maria decides that she has had enough, but feels that she can not tell Bastian. She urges Bastian to visit their physician, and she herself meets with a psychologist to talk about her problems.

Analysis of the situation

Bastian exhibits many characteristics of a gifted person. He is smart, enterprising, curious, a non-conformist and he puts all his energy into setting up his own company. But sometimes Bastian expresses his energy and talent primarily in negative ways. He provokes people with his behavior, takes unacceptable risks, especially when driving, and behaves unpredictably when angry. He is falling into the trap of excessive behavior. The situation is now tenuous. He behaves like a ticking time bomb.

Reflection on the situation

Bowing under Maria's pressure, Bastian agrees to visit their physician. He tells the doctor about his chest pains, but rejects the physician's suggestion that this situation might worsen because of the tension at home. He asks for a referral to a cardiologist, but the specialist finds nothing out-of-the-ordinary.

Maria proposes a last effort to save their marriage, asking Bastian to join her at the psychologist. She tells him that she wants to end their marriage. Though Bastian thinks there is nothing wrong with him, he eventually agrees to go along because Maria wants it so much and because he does not want to lose her.

This is the psychologist's description of the conversations with Bastian and Maria.

Dealing with obstructive thoughts

Bastian and his wife Maria arrive separately. Maria explains that Bastian didn't really want to come. Bastian immediately goes into attack mode, telling Maria to shut up. Only he will explain what is happening. He says that Maria takes no responsibility for the company; he has to do everything himself. He suggests his collaborator/partner should make sure she finds a replacement if she wants to do something else; she should not bother him.

On the other hand, if he has to go out, it should be understood that Maria will, of course, take care of customers and suppliers. Maria is surprised. She had never heard that before.

Speaking from her point of view, Maria complains that Bastian shows no interest in her. If she worries about one of their children, he never responds because he is always working on something. Bastian completely rejects her view and says that his wife complains constantly. "He never does anything right." And so both sides are playing the blame game. Maria says that all of her children want to move away as soon as possible because they can no longer bear the tension. Bastian rejects that as nonsense.

I ask them why they are here. There is a tension-filled silence. Maria tells me that I know her and what she wants. I tell her that I prefer to hear people use their own words to explain their goals. When they tell me their desires, I write them down. In this case I have trouble understanding what they want other than blaming each other. Maria wants a mate who listens to her, while Bastian wants a business partner who shares the responsibility. Both want things to quieten down.

After a few more conversations the list of desires has grown. But the sessions show an ever-repeating pattern of blame and dragging up the past. Bastian appears to have little insight into his own behavior and its effects. Maria takes everything as criticism. I decide to meet with them individually to discuss the relationship because I cannot see a way to break the pattern.

Dealing with emotions

When Bastian comes in by himself, he starts a very long story about an experience with a colleague. He has a lot of fun telling the anecdote, but only by himself. I suddenly see a different side of Bastian. He tells the story with humor and energy. I suggest that Bastian could easily join an improv theater group with his playful and lively way of telling a story, but I say I now want to talk with him about more serious matters.

Bastian falls silent and leans forward. Suddenly he says: "I don't want to lose Maria, but I feel desperate. I don't know what to do." He says that he had made a beautiful wooden sculpture for Maria, putting his heart and soul into it. He had put it in the room for her. But Maria didn't understand. She only wanted to know why he had given it to her. He became furious and put the sculpture back in the shed because she didn't understand his gesture. I notice that Bastian has difficulty expressing his 'soft' feelings. Though he does not want to lose Maria, he seems to express only anger. And that anger runs very deep, I think, because of the extreme way in which it is expressed. When I share that observation with Bastian, he denies it. I get the impression that Bastian is holding a great deal of old grief bottled up inside, grief that can be traced back to his relationship with his mother and sisters.

I tell Bastian that I believe he is gifted because he had the intelligence, energy and creativity to create a completely new, successful company. As a child he was very curious and explored the world on his own. His non-conforming behavior also fits this diagnosis.
The result of his high giftedness is that Bastian focuses on content and knows a lot. I explain that one of the pitfalls of being gifted may be that – because you know so much about the content – you think you are always right about the matter at hand and you conclude there is nothing wrong with you if there is a conflict. You don't have to change, but others should.
In the same way, Bastian blames others when something goes wrong, as he did with Maria. I ask if he ever thinks back to past conflicts with his wife. He says he does, but usually concludes that he is still in the right. During Bastian's storytelling I notice that he has very negative thoughts about himself. He doubts many of his actions. When I ask if he ever doubted his role as a husband, Bastian admits that he did, but thought everyone occasionally had those feelings. Just when I think I have made contact with him, he retreats.

When I point that out, Bastian does not recognize it. I am finding this a hard case and am not sure if Bastian may be helped more through psychotherapy.
I ask Bastian if he will object to my discussing this anonymously with a few colleagues. Bastian does not think it would be useful, but he agrees.

How to proceed?
The psychologist consults an occupational physician and a psychiatrist/psychotherapist with whom she forms a small group of experts.

The occupational physician
I think that it is a good thing this man started his own company. In a work situation with other people or with a different supervisor he could have snapped a long time ago. By the way, this is a known characteristic of gifted people. Maybe there are also life phase problems with this man. He is currently 53 and may have started to think about what he has really achieved in his life. I would certainly ask how his parents are. I also notice many problems in communicating, and I wonder if there is a borderline personality disorder. So I am curious what the psychiatrist/psychotherapist thinks.

The psychiatrist/psychotherapist
I recognize elements of a personality disorder, but I would first like to explore that with Bastian himself. That will probably not be easy because he has trouble accepting anything from another person. He probably also isn't motivated to make an appointment with me, I'm afraid.

The psychologist
I am a bit ambivalent about Bastian's situation. Sometimes he cannot be reached, denies everything and doesn't listen at all. Sometimes I also see an approachable side of him. At those moments he appears to be thinking of the havoc he creates with his anger and impatience.

He sometimes talks a bit about his youth. I still see remarkably few emotions, such as sadness and mourning. I think the fact that his wife drew a line in the sand is offering him an opportunity to change things. He doesn't want to lose her. Possibly the threat of a divorce must be turned into an actual separation before Bastian will seriously start working on himself. I have the impression that he has problems with women especially. His past might play a role in that. I think that Bastian has a long way to go. The most important condition for improvement in his situation will be his desire to work on his problems.

During our next conversation I tell Bastian what we discussed in the group of experts. I give him a couple of choices. He can continue doing what he is doing. In that case, his wife will probably decide to divorce him. However, if Bastian chooses professional guidance, there are a number of possibilities. He can start working on his relationship with his wife with my help, as his psychologist.
But it doesn't appear this is the only approach for Bastian's problems. Therefore it seems advisable for Bastian to first do some self-analysis. If it is established that he is gifted, this may help him form a more positive self-image. In that case he may work more intensely to overcome these negative patterns. I propose to Bastian that he makes an appointment with a psychiatrist. He or she can then help investigate elements of personality problems.
But he may also suffer from depression or chronic overexertion (or burnout, see the information chapter) because Bastian is so tired and listless. The psychiatrist's analysis will guide Bastian to find an effective approach to his problems. Bastian needs some time to think this over, and says he will call me later.

9. Everybody is against me....

Rose Fisher, 36, grew up with three other siblings, all girls, in a single-family house in a pleasant suburb. Both of her parents graduated from law school. Her father became a prominent lawyer, and though her mother opted not to practice law, she became an active volunteer while managing their household very meticulously.
Rose was a child after her mother's heart: she was a very exacting, neat and happy child until she reached puberty. She was an excellent student. Because she always wanted to excel, she spent a lot of time on her homework. Her mother helped Rose with translating Greek and Latin, but often became impatient because Rose needed more time to understand the texts than she did.
Rose began to resent her mother's help and became convinced that she wasn't good enough in her mother's eyes. She increasingly withdrew to her room where she would spend hours dressing up. As a child, Rose spent a lot of time with her older sister Claire, but during puberty she withdrew from her sisters, focusing more on reading and corresponding with girls abroad. As a result, Rose – whose native language is Dutch – learned to speak and write French and English very well. She also shows great musical talent, is able to play any instrument she is given and sings very well. Eventually she learned to play the piano and to play well because she practiced all the time.

After graduating from high school, Rose decided to study French and history and to attend a music college. To prepare, she took lessons from a new piano teacher, a Russian woman who demanded much from her students. Rose often broke out in a cold sweat when she had a lesson. According to her teacher, Rose never did anything right, but Rose felt she could not withdraw from her lessons because she thought that would make her teacher sad.

She was reluctant to have a conversation with her instructor about the way she taught.

At the same time, Rose began her university studies, but her history study went wrong very quickly. She seemed unable to master the details of what had happened in the past and also didn't understand the main concepts. Her French courses began poorly as well. Rose's mother was deeply disappointed because she had such high expectations of her. Her sisters, after graduating from high school, had gone directly to their careers. One of her sisters became a medical specialist, another was a successful opera singer and the youngest was studying to become an accountant. When she started college, Rose moved out of her parents' house. Because she came from a wealthy family, she was used to living in style. Her parents thought that Rose needed to learn how to deal with money, so they gave her only a small allowance. Because Rose enjoyed having good clothes and dressing well, she decided to get jobs through a temp agency. She found work in a lawyer's office (with a bit of help from her father) and worked as a secretary for one of the partners.

Rose did her best to please her supervisor. Everything was perfectly taken care of. But because she did everything very thoroughly, she worked fairly slowly. Because she got along well with her supervisor and did good work, she thought that she deserved a higher salary than her colleagues. Rose quickly developed a reputation as being conceited. She thought that was ridiculous. "All those girls are jealous and that is why they bully me." Rose became increasingly isolated at work. Her supervisor concluded that she was unwilling to keep working until everything was finished, which took a long time since she worked slowly. He got tired of her constant requests for more money, so he fired her. At that point something snaps. Rose believes she has done everything possible to fulfill her responsibilities, producing flawless English and French translations and receiving clients graciously, better than anyone else. And now this! She doesn't understand and believes it is very unfair.

Rose has abandoned her studies of French, so she needs to find a different job. She decides to begin teaching French in a high school, but that, too, is a disaster. Not surprisingly, Rose developed an excellent, creative lesson program, but she does not connect to her students' interests. She considers them disrespectful boors with no interest in culture. She is fired even before completing her trial period. She tries again, this time as a librarian. There, too, she soon has conflicts with her colleagues. Rose wants to satisfy the customers and often accompanies them to find a book. Because of that, she does not have enough time to complete her own work. She criticizes her colleagues: one is not accurate; the next one is rude to the visitors; a third one makes mistakes, etc. Rose often expresses her feelings in public and is fired yet again.

While working in the lawyer's office, Rose met a partner in a large accounting office. She was very much in love and they quickly decided to marry. Her husband, Rudolph, is a very educated man, 10 years Rose's senior. He loves having meetings at home where people talk about current subjects related to his area of expertise. Rose is well suited to plan these activities and organizes the meetings down to the smallest details. She also believes that she can participate in the discussions, since she has gone to college. Her husband disagrees, and they fight.

Rose has invested a lot of work to design their new house, painting and furnishing it very tastefully. She begins to take piano lessons again, and initially everything seems to be going well. But Rose's contact with the neighbors deteriorates quickly. They live close to the neighbors in a semi-detached house. She feels that these neighbors make too much noise, play their radios too loud. Rose is angry: why do they do that to her? In turn, the neighbors bang on the wall when Rose plays the piano. Likewise, Rose does not enjoy a good relationship with her in-laws. She criticizes everyone and even goes so far as to forbid Rudolph from visiting his family.

When Rudolph refuses, Rose holds that against him, saying he deserts her. The two of them disagree about children: Rose does not want children and Rudolph does. The marriage lasts only four years. During the divorce proceedings, Rose fights for every last penny of her share. She believes she is entitled, because Rudolph left her.

Rose ends up alone, again. She works at one job after another, but always ends up in the same position. Rose always appeals her firings, but never wins. She thinks that is very unfair. Everybody is always against her.

Finally, when she is 36, Rose secures a job at an international beauty product sales organization. She is very dedcated to her work, but soon enough she quarrels with one of her colleagues, accusing him of talking behind her back and using her translations. Rose even writes to her supervisor saying that she did the translation and not her colleague. After that incident, Rose finds it strange that her colleague does not want to talk to her any more.

Because her super-visor is impressed with Rose's knowledge of English and French and her talent for organization, he does not want to lose her for the organization. So he suggests her to ask for coaching in order to work on her communication skills.
Rose rejects this idea forcefully. If there is one person with good communication skills, it is her. No coaching. Her supervisor tells her that she has to accept the help; otherwise he will have to take other measures. Rose feels that she is now forced to visit a coach....

Analysis of the situation
Rose's father and mother are probably gifted, and her sisters' careers also point in that direction. In this family, being smart is 'normal.' As a result, Rose does not stand out as a gifted child. Although Rose is likely also gifted, she does not realize it herself.

As a result, she falls into a number of traps - trivializing her own faults, blaming others and pointing out procedures that are poorly executed. Rose is angry at the whole world. The world doesn't understand her, gossips about her, is jealous of her and, above all, is unfair. Her reactions seem to repeat themselves, becoming ever more compulsive. She is a perfectionist, suspects everyone, and fears failure. It appears she has little insight into her own role in all of this.

Reflection on the situation
Rose visits a coach. The coach describes what happens.

Dealing with obstructive thoughts and emotions
Because Rose's supervisor gives her no other options, she must meet with a coach. As a result she enters my office in a huff and immediately asks what I think I can do for her. She says that I should talk to her supervisor, and then I will understand her. Next, Rose shares a long list of accusations against her colleague and a list of everything she did right. I want to hear more about what gives her such pride in her work; she is able to explain that very well.
I also sense what she finds important, primarily respect and good relationships. When I ask Rose what she contributes to those relationships, she says: "Everything." I leave that alone for the moment. She also talks a bit about her family circumstances.

I ask if she ever had an intelligence test. She says she had been tested and had scored 146. I tell her that this score makes her highly gifted. Rose is not at all surprised, but she seems happy with the fact. I don't think that Rose has done anything with these talents. She looks for affirmation through all the things she thinks she does right. She appears to be very afraid and suspicious. I wonder if I should refer her to a psychotherapist, but I think she is not ready, since she has so little insight into her own behavior. I am afraid that she will see my proposal as a lack of respect. Therefore I postpone this suggestion for the moment.

Next, I show her a picture of the brain with all kinds of out-side connections. I ask Rose for her connections. What con-nections does she have with the things and/or people around her, including her work, new piano teacher, and her mother who divorced her father and whom she usually visits during the holidays? Rose has very few other contacts. I think that she is very lonely, but I do not see a reaction when I bring up that observation.

At the end of the conversation I ask Rose what she thinks of it. She says that she certainly likes me, but that she does not think she can learn anything from me, certainly regard-ing communication skills, as her supervisor wanted. There-fore, she says she does not want to come back.

Because I am concerned about her future, I decide to raise the possibility of referring her to a psychotherapist.
I describe a number of her behaviors, such as her fears, suspicions, and compulsive way of dealing with things. I tell Rose that I suspect she has some (not all) characteristics of a personality disorder (see text box) but I explain I cannot explore this further because I am not a psychotherapist. Rose listens, but says that regarding her personality I am completely wrong. She is not at fault, she says, the cause is her environment.

What is a personality disorder?
A personality disorder is a set of innate characteris-tics that cause a person to react based on the cir-cumstances in which he/she was raised. Childhood experiences and reactions of other persons can cause problems under certain circumstances. Those per-sonal characteristics and experiences influence someone's whole life.
The official psychiatric manual, the DSM-IV (Diagnos-tic and Statistical Manual of the American Psychiatric Association, Fourth Edition), defines a personality disorder as a lasting pattern of inner experience and

behavior that differs markedly from the expectations of the individual's culture, is pervasive and inflexible, starts in adolescence or early adulthood, is stable over time, and leads to distress or impairment. Personality disorders are a long-standing and maladaptive pattern of perceiving and responding to other people and to stressful circumstances.

A week later, I am surprised when she calls. She asks me what I really think about her personality problems. I tell her that I hope she will agree to being diagnosed by a psychotherapist. If Rose agrees, I tell her that very effective help is available for these kinds of problems. Rose says she has researched personality disorders on the Internet. She thinks she may suffer from something like this, because her husband has said similar things. At the time she did not dare pursue this possibility with her family doctor because she feared she would then really get in trouble.

I tell her that I am happy to help her find a good psychotherapist if she wants, and that I will look for someone knowledgeable about the gifted. Rose says goodbye rather distantly, but I believe that my offer did touch her.

How to proceed?
After a serious incident at work, Rose calls in sick. Her boss is ready to fire her. Rose shows signs of extensive strain and is told to report to the occupational physician.

The occupational physician
Rose comes to me with her story of being a 'jack of all trades' and master of none. She says that she called in sick and that her employer wants to fire her.

I immediately think of this as a labor dispute, incompatibility between employer and employee. But is this a real illness? Talking to her I notice that there really may be something wrong with her. Her story reveals many fears and a great deal of compulsive behavior, and I suspect that this may be a case of a personality issue. Rose shares that the coach, whom she has visited at her boss' insistence, concluded something similar. That only increases her fear because she really does not know what to do. I am also unsure about how to proceed and with Rose's permission I submit the case to my peer group of experts, composed of a psychiatrist, a Work and Organizational psychologist and a career coach.

To recap

The occupational physician submits the case to her expert group and receives the following responses:

The psychiatrist

I think there might be a personality issue, but I can only confirm this after a number of conversations and tests. Because Rose never asked for psychiatric help, a real personality disorder is unlikely, but there may be some characteristics of a personality disorder. This might explain Rose's feelings that everybody is against her. If that is the case, it will be difficult to motivate Rose to work on her problems by herself. However, I think that it might be worth pursuing this in light of Rose's current problems. I know a number of recently developed therapies that I would like to use in this case, including forms of cognitive behavioral therapy that have proven very effective. But they are very intense and must be continued for a long time. A combination with coaching, and focusing on work, seems useful to me.

The Work and Organizational psychologist

I can start working with Rose as soon as the exact problem is identified. It must be clear whether she exhibits any characteristics of a personality disorder.

Perhaps the psychiatrist could start working with her on that while I, as a psychologist, play more of a coaching role and guide Rose in her work, if her employer is willing to give Rose another chance. For example, I would be willing to talk to Rose's supervisor together with her. This might contribute to a shared assessment of Rose's strong capabilities. And we might be able, during this three-party discussion, to see if there might be opportunities for Rose to move to other jobs and work environments. This exploration might lead to new opportunities.

The career coach
I think it will be difficult for Rose to gather enough courage to investigate what is going on in her life and what she really wants. I think that she also needs additional counseling for herself and in her work. I see some opportunities because she is also gifted.

The occupational physician submits her findings to Rose, who becomes confused and scared. The occupational physician expected this and asks if the Work and Organizational psychologist could make time for Rose right away and repeats her offer to help. During the conversation Rose calms down a bit.

With the aid of the occupational physician and the offer of help from the Work and Organizational psychologist, she feels less alone in her work and decides to talk to her supervisor together with the psychologist. She also wants to consult with a career coach, because she applied for a number of positions and that is becoming an increasing problem. She is applying for jobs that do not fit with her intelligence level.
With the help of a career coach, she may investigate what she really wants. Rose has not yet decided if she wants to pursue the possibility of a personality disorder diagnosis. She finds that too threatening, she says.

10. That's just the way I am!

Boris Vogel, 35, works at a library, the most recent of a number of short-term positions that have lasted only one or two years. Currently, Boris is on the brink of being fired again; his situation doesn't look good. He called in sick because he cannot deal with the situation any more.

Actually, Boris has always been the odd man out. His colleagues call him an eccentric or a weirdo. He looks the part – his clothing looks filthy and his personal hygiene isn't too good either, he always smells of sweat. When colleagues visit him at home they are shocked: the house is jampacked with stuff everywhere.
He collects all kinds of things, and makes a big mess. Old newspapers are everywhere, as are empty bottles and milk cartons, creating a horrible smell. Boris also expresses that he is not fond of receiving people at home.

At school Boris was also an outsider. He looked unkempt and didn't have any friends. He didn't mind too much, he wanted to have time for the many things that interested him, such as collecting old books. He made good grades. But he forgot simple things and he always lost everything. At the age that boys in his class started going to parties and became interested in girls, Boris spent most of his time at home with his books. Boris appreciated that he could talk to his father, a professor at a technical college, about his interests. His sister thought he was strange, but she did try to help him when he was being teased at school.
He graduated from high school at 17 and then went to study literature in college. But within a year he realized he was in the wrong place. Boris studied, but he also went to museums, read books, and scrounged around in flea markets. Eventually, he stopped taking his exams. When his parents refused to continue to pay for his studies, he took jobs in a

series of offices, first as a temp worker and after that a few years at an insurance company. Currently he has been working at a library for two years. The same pattern always develops at the places Boris works: he starts well, quickly understands the work, and then becomes distracted with other things because he gets bored quickly. His collecting habit satisfies his urge to start something new often. At work, his desk quickly becomes very chaotic and his work suffers. He is unable to finish his work, and according to his boss, he becomes dysfunctional. He can talk about anything, knows all the details, but he just fails to complete his real work. However, he has invented a whole new registration system on his own and he writes an informational booklet about the library, projects that no one at the library had asked him to do. His supervisor and colleagues find him inscrutable. They try everything they can think of to bring him in line, but there is no real connection.

After various attempts to do this by all sides, his supervisor gives him a very poor evaluation, which Boris cannot understand. The criticism focuses on his way of working, bringing up too many irrelevant issues, and failing to complete his assignments. Boris seems completely indifferent to the criticism and continues doing things his own way, ignoring suggestions to improve the way he works. During the last conversation with the supervisor, Boris suddenly realizes that his job is at risk. The supervisor now tells him that they want to fire him, because he is completely dysfunctional. That greatly worries Boris and causes many problems (including physical issues). He calls in sick a few days later.

Analysis of the situation

For a long time, Boris has not functioned well in a variety of jobs. He shows eccentric behavior and does not take good care of himself. At home, he just gets by, with some help. He believes that this is just the way he is, and does not understand why everybody always criticizes him. Now, they even want to fire him. Because he called in sick, his supervisor orders him to visit the occupational physician.

Although he was never tested at school and no one has ever said so, many characteristics suggest that Boris may be gifted. He has many interests, is only involved with content and he doesn't pay any attention to his appearance. He is able to discuss a broad range of topics, and knows all kinds of details. Boris himself is not aware of possibly being gifted.

At the same time, he lacks the basic skills to function well in society and in a workplace, including the ability to reflect on his own behavior in relation to his environment. This combination causes Boris to have ongoing issues. The situation is now quite serious.

Reflection on the situation

Boris makes an appointment with the occupational physician.

The occupational physician

When Boris meets me two weeks after calling in sick, I have already received some information about him from the supervisor through the social-medical team[5]. We discuss Boris' complaints. He says that he is not doing well, experiences headaches and sleeps badly. I ask about his job and whether it is the main source of the problem. Boris indicates that he receives much criticism, but that he does not know what he should do differently. That's the way he is.

I note from his body language that he is anxious, and sits uneasily in his chair, avoiding my eyes when I look at him. He is hardly able to express himself and also sweats heavily. I try to put him at ease by giving him a glass of water and make a casual observation about the room we are in, on the 19th floor, and the beautiful view. He relaxes a bit and tells me exactly which buildings he recognizes.

---

5   The social medical team talks about people on (longer) sick leave and consists of the personnel officer, the occupational physician and the head of the employee's department.

I then decide to ask him about his life. In answer to my questions, he tells me that he lives alone and has never had a relationship. He does have some contact with his parents, but he does not have a very good relationship with his father. His father criticizes him a lot. (He tells this story in a soft, monotonous voice with no apparent feeling.) His mother drops by once in a while and helps him clean his house a bit. His sister visits infrequently to help with housekeeping.

I think that currently Boris is unable to work. However, I feel a bit torn, is this person unable to work for medical reasons? How can I continue working on this, how can I follow the problem from my position as an occupational physician? And what advice do I give the employer who clearly wants to fire this man?
I decide first to ask for advice from the Work and Organizational psychologist I have worked with before once in a while. I also ask if the psychologist wants to check whether Boris is exhibiting a psychopathology, especially: could this be a case of an autism spectrum disorder and/or a personality disorder?

The Work and Organizational psychologist talks with Boris and recognizes elements of an autism spectrum disorder, but because she is not an expert in this area, she advises me to contact a clinical psychologist or psychiatrist. Boris is not very eager to cooperate, but he understands that he basically has no choice.

The clinical psychologist has two extensive conversations with Boris and has him perform a number of tests. She checks various areas with him and writes a report that she submits to Boris and the occupational physician. The report includes the following items.

Dealing with obstructive thoughts
Boris does not understand how problems always appear in his work. He thinks this always happen *to* him. He thinks that he

tries his best, and that is why he is so surprised when he receives the negative evaluation. He continues emphasizing that 'this is just the way he is' and that he cannot change just like that. The psychologist does not succeed in helping him look at his situation from another point of view. She does notice that he seems to exhibit signs of very high intelligence and proposes that he takes an IQ test. She has to encourage him to do the test. The test shows that he is indeed highly intelligent. His performance IQ is 157 and his verbal IQ is 120. In addition, using tests, the psychologist establishes that there is a slight disorder in the autism spectrum; Asperger's syndrome seems to be the most likely conclusion.

Dealing with emotions
Sorting out Boris' emotions is a challenge – even he cannot explain them. He says that he is shocked by his supervisor's intent to fire him. He didn't see that coming. He is very sad, and also angry, but he finds it hard to express these feelings. When I press him on this subject Boris says he feels hurt and not recognized for the efforts he puts in for the company. After all, he did work on a new registration system and an informational booklet about the library, didn't he? Now his supervisor wants to fire him! It causes him to clam up completely. And it causes headaches and heart palpitations. He cannot do anything anymore. He is very downcast and hardly eats or sleeps.

Motivation
Boris' motivation to work at the library was that he could spend the whole day among books. If he wants to look up something, he can also do that fast. He likes working there and he would be very upset if he could not return. He wonders if he can work anywhere else. But for the moment he does not want to do anything at all. He had never experienced such feelings.

Psychopathology
The clinical psychologist thinks that Boris may have an adaptive disorder based on his high intelligence, something that hasn't been discovered until now. He also has a large verbal-performance gap. In gifted people we often see such verbal-performance gaps. By itself this is not the cause of problems, but sometimes because of them there might be a lack of balance in development.

This large verbal–performance gap could partly explain why Boris is unsuccessful socially. Although there is no consensus by experts it is assumed that with such a gap (more than 12 points difference between the two kinds of intelligence), a person cannot transfer the data from one area to the other very well.
It may also explain why Boris didn't finish college and why he allows so much physical chaos at home and at work.
Here is some information on Asperger's syndrome, in the Information chapter we provide more information about autism in general.

Asperger's syndrome
Asperger's syndrome is seen as a disorder in the autism spectrum. The syndrome is named after pediatrician Hans Asperger who studied and described children in his practice who lacked nonverbal communication skills, demonstrated limited empathy with their peers, and were physically clumsy.

Most people with autism have a low intelligence. It is unclear whether Asperger's syndrome overlaps with high functioning autism. There is also a debate whether Asperger's syndrome is really part of the autism spectrum. Some people have suggested that gifted people with a verbal-performance gap show similar characteristics. Others think that gifted people who had problems adjusting as a child show autistic behavior.

People who are gifted and have characteristics of a disorder in the autism spectrum have a high need of order and predictability.

Diagnosing this is difficult: in adults and in gifted people. Diagnosing disorders in the autism spectrum is very difficult. There is a lack of scientific knowledge of this group of people. There certainly is a grey zone (Burger-Veltmeijer, 2007). We often see they need specialized help, which is hard to find.

How to proceed?
Using the report by the clinical psychologist, the occupational physician outlines the possible actions together with Boris.

Practical assistance
Boris can receive practical assistance from a regional organization that supports people with psychiatric disorders. A social worker will help him get his life in order. It is also advisable for the social worker to contact someone who knows something about high giftedness, because this also could influence Boris' behavior.
Boris likes the idea of practical assistance by a professional because he never really liked to rely on his mother's and sister's assistance, he was actually a bit ashamed of it.

Work
Under the circumstances, chances are slim that Boris can return to his old job. That would be unfortunate because Boris feels comfortable there. There might be specific and difficult problems, but the occupational physician would like to investigate whether there are other opportunities for him in the library. She will do this in consultation with Boris' supervisor and Boris himself.

Because she also wonders if Boris is employable in a 'normal' work environment, in light of his behavior, the experiences at work in various positions and the psychologist's diagnosis, she asks a friend who is an insurance physician[6] whether *theoretically* Boris might be eligible for disability payments.

The insurance physician
In order to qualify for disability payments, there must be a disability of a 'direct and objectively medically determinable' nature, i.e. caused by an illness or a handicap. To the extent that Boris suffers from disabilities, and they definitely seem to exist, these must be the result of an illness. The insurance physician will list those restrictions in the so-called List of Functional Opportunities. Such a list must include restrictions in functioning as a person and in society.

Some items in the list where Boris might score low, based on the Asperger's Syndrome and the verbal-performance gap, include: being able to react flexibly to often changing performance conditions and/or tasks, dealing with failures and disruptions and deadlines or production peaks, and dealing with other people's emotional problems and with conflicts. A major question is whether Boris will be able to perform a task as part of a group. He will probably not score very well on the item 'cooperation.' He might even need work that usually doesn't require direct contact with colleagues, not to mention close supervision. So, it remains a question whether Boris might be able to function 'properly' in a 'normal' work situation.

---

6   An insurance physician in the Netherlands works for the UWV (Worker's Insurance Authority) to assesses the ability to work in the position after two years of sick leave and provides medical reasons to determine whether a disability pension is granted. If someone is partially or fully incapable of working in his or her position he or she may be eligible to receive benefits under the Work and Income Act (WIA).

In addition, there is still the problem that, in order to qualify for a disability payment, Boris must experience limits resulting from an illness. Being 'gifted' is not an illness, but may be seen as a personal character trait, which creates more risks that people will be unable to work under certain conditions. Some gifted people can fall apart because of problems including mood, fear or somatic disorders. If that happens, or if there is a major chance that this will happen, the insurance physician may indicate that there are long-term work limits. That may be part of what applies here. The combination with Asperger's syndrome does limit job opportunities.

Whether Boris will be eligible for disability payments will depend on the occupational assessor[7]. If he or she would be able to find jobs that Boris could still perform despite all of his limitations, Boris' original salary will be compared to the average for the suitable positions, which will then determine the disability percentage.

Sometimes the occupational assessor may find too few jobs or none at all. In that case, Boris would be considered fully disabled. As expected, Boris does not like to be labeled 'disabled' and to collect a benefit. He would prefer to continue searching for opportunities in his current position together with the occupational physician, his personnel manager and his supervisor.

To recap
The occupational physician discusses her experiences with Boris with a colleague in her peer group of experts.

The occupational physician
I hope that it is too early to apply for a disability allowance and that suitable work can be found for Boris in his current job.

---

7   The occupational assessor works with the insurance physician looking for positions that might suit the client taking into account his or her limits.

Wouldn't there be a place somewhere for a person with his talents? I will propose that the employer contact a coach with experience of people with a disorder in the autism spectrum. I am sure that practical assistance should be arranged for Boris first. Then we should assess his situation again and find out what is the best way for him to fill his days with activities he is able to do and which are good (and not harmful) for him. Some people with autism are extremely talented in a special field. On the other hand, these people sometimes find it impossible to work in an organization or in a group. They will very quickly become too stressed and unfit for work. I hope we can save Boris for the labor market.

I expect he needs special assistance for the rest of his working life and his employer should be educated about Boris' character traits and what is needed to allow him to work there. Maybe Boris can be placed in a special project where people with autism are given jobs that suit them and receive counseling at the same time.

11. I can't choose...

**Malcolm Jacobs is a 33 year-old teacher of economics
and history at a high school in the town of Nijmegen in the
Netherlands. Life has not been going very well for him
lately: he has trouble sleeping and shows signs of
overstrain.**

When he was a child, his parents, especially his mother,
noticed that Malcolm was highly intelligent. He could read
before he went to kindergarten, because he followed
closely what his sister did, who was two years older. He
taught himself to add and subtract and almost by accident
discovered negative numbers. He read everything he could
get his hands on and asked questions about everything.
Malcolm was also a physically active child, but that didn't
bother his parents. They themselves were not quiet people,
and Malcolm was not a difficult child for them.

Malcolm was sufficiently engaged at home because there
was a lot of space (literally and figuratively). He had an
older brother and sister who often spent time with him.
When he was about seven years old, Malcolm became
depressed and his mother looked for help. Malcolm took
intelligence tests that determined he was gifted, which
wasn't a surprise to his parents.
Malcolm's mother explained to him in a way that he could
understand that his brain just worked a little faster than
the brains of other children and, as a result, he thought
about things a lot. She talked with his school about the
findings, because his teacher had already mentioned that
she was concerned during parent-teacher meetings. The
teacher found Malcolm to be a difficult child because he
would be very quiet for a while and then suddenly become
very active.

He needed to get help, and the parents had to arrange that themselves. The school was not responsible. The teacher did not think that Malcolm's problem was being gifted, but that his behavior was.

A number of conversations with a child psychologist offered no help since he was not familiar with high giftedness and thought Malcolm's issue was more like ADHD. Malcolm's mother decided to stop asking for help and started her own research. With the knowledge she collected about gifted children, Malcolm's mother thought that she could support her son perfectly well herself. After that, he didn't have trouble in school regarding his performance. He was depressed from time to time, but those periods did not last very long. His mother believed that Malcolm became depressed when he was bored. If she let him do something new, the depression went away by itself.

Malcolm graduated from high school and went on to study history. After two years he decided to add economics to his studies. He also took up acting and was active in a fraternity. Still, sometimes Malcolm experienced difficult periods. Fortunately, he could talk to his mother about many things and he felt that he did not need professional help.

After six years Malcolm graduated from university with two degrees but no idea what he was going to do. A former classmate worked as an English teacher, so he decided to look into teaching. He applied for a half-time job and started writing articles on the side. He also considered writing a book. Malcolm rather liked teaching. He had good relationships with his students and was known for telling colorful stories.

Initially things went well. But after a few years of teaching, his colleagues noticed that Malcolm was becoming increasingly erratic. He still prepared his lessons, but the quantity of materials he collected for lessons kept growing. He was becoming almost obsessive in his conduct, they thought. The classroom cupboards started bulging and nobody, including

Malcolm himself, knew exactly what was inside and where everything was stored. Malcolm had also become a member of the school's advisory council and was the mentor of a class. He was also a member of a working group for the gifted (where he fought for good psychological care for gifted children) and worked with the school's theater club as a director. In addition he had joined a theater group and often played the lead in its annual play. He also had many friends with whom he socialized.

And he regularly wrote articles for a national daily about current affairs. He started thinking about going into politics. His private life also became increasingly hectic. Where once he had trouble finding a girlfriend, during the last couple of years he had a different girlfriend every year, though he noticed that they always left him after a while. But he did not see that as a real problem, so he never talked to an ex-girlfriend about their relationship.

Inside his apartment the chaos grew. He bought all kinds of books about different subjects that seemed interesting. He read them, but then did not put them away properly. He cut articles from the paper about subjects that interested him and which he wanted to use as reference for his own articles, but he didn't know how to store them, so the clippings were everywhere. He did not clean his apartment much because he just did not enjoy cleaning. So his apartment gradually became very dirty. Once when a colleague visited him at home, Malcolm remained standing in the door because he really didn't dare let that colleague come inside.

Malcolm increasingly can't sleep and he begins to arrive at school tired and irritated. When the head of the history department, John Slope, tries to talk to him one morning about how things are going, Malcolm starts shaking and says that he is not feeling very well. At that moment he has strong heart palpitations and pain in his chest. John becomes worried and takes Malcolm to the doctor. An initial examination doesn't show anything out of the ordinary. The physician thinks that Malcolm has had a panic attack and talks that over with him.

When Malcolm says that his complaints started at work, the physician asks a little more about his situation. Malcolm explains that things are not going well, and the physician advises him to make an appointment with the occupational physician soon.

Analysis of the situation

Malcolm exhibits many characteristics of being gifted, which he has known for a long time because he was tested when he was a child. He is interested in many things and also quickly learns a lot about a subject. That is a major advantage for his work as a teacher. However, that can also be a pitfall. Because he finds everything interesting he has difficulties choosing only one subject to explore further. As a result, he loses his grip on his own life. He manages to do many things at once, but cannot organize his work. The same goes for his private life. In his head, the chaos also increases, making him restless and that leads to him trying to do more and more. His behavior shows ADHD-like signs *(see the information chapter)*.

Malcolm chose teaching because, in that position, he would be able to do more for gifted children than his own teachers did for him.

Reflection on the situation

At John Slope's urging, Malcolm calls in sick and makes an appointment with the occupational physician within a week. She reports the following about the consultation.

The occupational physician
Malcolm is very relieved when he notes that I know about the gifted. The questions and problems he presents to me are:

- There is chaos in my head and in my home. What can I do about that?

- My family doctor thinks that I might have ADHD. What do you think about that? Is that also the reason for my heart problems?
- Actually I should make more decisions in my work and private life, but I'm afraid I will become depressed if I don't have enough challenges. That happened in the past a number of times. What should I do about that?
- I do have girlfriends but they always leave. How can I build stronger relationships?

Despite his continuing problems, Malcolm wants to return to work a week later. Before that, I propose that he first thinks about how he can address the chaos in his life. And I ask him if he wants to be examined to see if he has ADHD. Malcolm agrees to that. I make an appointment for him with a psychiatrist, someone who also knows about the gifted. I advise him to read about ADHD in a book I lend him, so that he can prepare himself. He can also look on the internet, for instance at http://www.mayoclinic.com health/adult-adhd/ DS01161. I ask him to call me the following week to let me know how he is doing and to discuss returning to work. I also propose that he has an exploratory conversation with a Work and Organizational psychologist about his questions, about the choices he would like to make at work.

The Work and Organizational psychologist
Malcolm tells me that he has trouble organizing his work. He likes working on many subjects at the same time, but, in education, that means that he has to do many things by himself. He has problems with that. He wonders what this has to do with his giftedness, or with ADHD. He also questions everything. Is he in the right place? Does he have to choose? If yes, on what should he base his choices? Won't he become depressed if he starts working less hard? What about his private relationships? Why do his girlfriends leave him? Malcolm is busy dealing with a lot of questions in his head.

I propose that he starts by working on everything in steps. Before we address his questions, I propose to Malcolm that he first organize his apartment and find out if he has ADHD. Then, those questions at least would be answered. In order to organize his apartment I will check which organizations can help him with that. As the occupational physician had already arranged, Malcolm will visit a psychiatrist who is also knowledgeable about giftedness, to take the ADHD tests. Malcolm agrees with the proposals and visits the psychiatrist.

The psychiatrist

Based on the ADHD criteria *(see information chapter)* I conclude that Malcolm indeed has ADHD symptoms. I propose he starts to use medication. Malcolm discusses the advantages and disadvantages of the medication. He considers it an advantage that it will quiet all of the activity in his head. He would like that. Maybe it will make it easier for him to make choices. But he is afraid that he would no longer be 'himself.' And he will have to take medications his whole life. Malcolm considers everything quietly; another person who has gone through that process himself lends him a booklet and he does some reading about the pros and cons. Then he decides to try the medication. I also offer Malcolm the practical assistance of a social psychiatric nurse to help organize his house. And I advise Malcolm to talk about his work with the Work and Organizational psychologist.

Malcolm decides to visit the Work and Organizational psychologist a couple of times. He also accepts the offer to help organize his apartment with a social psychiatric nurse. In consultation with the occupational physician, he decides he will work part-time during the first couple of weeks to give himself time to relax physically and to arrange his life while getting used to the medications.

How to proceed?

Malcolm makes a list for himself of what he will do now.

Clean up his apartment

He asks for assistance from a social psychiatric nurse to clean his apartment and to learn to manage his household. That is a relief for him, because he could not see how to do this for himself. The nurse also teaches him all kinds of tricks to keep matters manageable and not let them slide. Initially he schedules frequent visits, but quickly decreases that frequency to once a month.

Conversations with the Work and Organizational psychologist

Malcolm says that he is feeling more at ease because of the medications. His heart palpitations have disappeared, but he still feels very tired. He also has returned to working part-time, though he reports feeling very anxious. When I drill a little deeper, he says that he is especially afraid of becoming depressed again and does not want to return to his bad memories of that condition. At those times, he felt as if he didn't have control over his life. His mother always arranged everything for him. How is he supposed to do that all by himself? His fear prevents him from calmly thinking about his current situation.

Together we discuss how he can channel his fear. First, Malcolm will need structure, so we decide that he shall initially look at his job. Malcolm needs a lot of time to arrange numerous small tasks, such as buying material for his lessons, making copies, etc. The possibility that he will forget all kinds of things is making him restless. In consultation with John Slope, we seek a temporary solution that gives Malcolm peace. At Malcolm's request, we decide to wait to address the underlying questions about his fears and his relationships. The fact that he has started working on his questions step by step calms him down and he wants to keep it that way.

Contacts at work

While Malcolm is working part-time, he has trouble delegating part of his work to colleagues. Fortunately, his colleagues and the head of his department are very sympathetic. John Slope arranges for him to receive temporary administrative support so that he can organize all his books, articles, and materials. Because his colleagues really like Malcolm, they try to support him as much as possible. John asks him for advice regarding a new lesson program and Malcolm really enjoys that work. He discusses with John the possibility of doing more lesson development for the whole department. But will he then not miss his students? For a moment Malcolm is again bothered by his old problem: not being able to choose. Malcolm thinks that he has to make a decision, but John explains that one thing can easily be combined with another.

Motivation

During this time Malcolm thinks about changing his job. Is that what he wants? Did he really choose this? He does not know. He likes his job, but class sizes are growing and increasingly he has to organize things by himself. He considers discussing this further with a career coach who also has experience with the gifted.

Relationships

Malcolm is still reluctant to examine why his girlfriends always leave him. He hopes that once most of the mess in his apartment is cleaned up, this will improve. Malcolm has heard about Internet dating sites for people with a higher education. A sister of one of his colleagues made an excellent contact through that system. Malcolm starts looking if that might be an option for him.

To recap
The occupational physician and the Work and Organizational psychologist discuss Malcolm's situation.

The combination of giftedness and ADHD is a very difficult one. People who have both conditions are very inspired in their work, but their restlessness and mental chaos make them susceptible to overstrain and/or exhaustion. That is what happened to Malcolm. Thanks to his department head, he did not suffer a burnout, although he did have a fair number of complaints (related to work stress). Using practical assistance and medication, he managed to get his life back on track because the organization where Malcolm works shows much understanding and cooperation, looking for practical solutions to reduce his stress. His department head was also willing to look for work where Malcolm could apply his talents.

We noted that Malcolm, while seeking solutions to these problems, had already made many choices about what he does and does not want. With the aid of the people around him he is working on restoring his balance. A visit with a career coach can further help him find the source of his inspiration and his passion, which will make it easier for him to make choices during the rest of his life.

12. Gifted workers, hitting the target

A closer look
In this book we describe eleven examples of gifted adults and their challenges in adapting to their work environments. In this chapter, authors Noks Nauta and Sieuwke Ronner take a look back at these stories through the lens of their own professional backgrounds.

Especially striking is that many of these gifted individuals initially appeared like 'unguided missiles' when they went off course. Yet, fortunately, most were able to get back on the right path. Our cases consistently reveal issues in the work environment that encouraged these gifted individuals to think about their situations and to look for new ways forward. In this chapter we provide our view of this search process. How do gifted individuals lose their equilibrium? Why do so many of the gifted look like 'unguided missiles' in these situations? And how does such an unguided missile get back on course?

Abilities and traps
A gifted person possesses a special gift: the opportunity to perform great feats. The basis of this gift lies in the brain's physiology (and possibly also its anatomy). A person possessing such a multifaceted and powerful brain faces a huge challenge: how to use these gifts? Not all gifted people succeed, as our examples illustrate. Some gifted people become entangled in psychological traps that hide their special talents. In the eyes of their environment all that remains is a hard to manage, difficult person, as so dramatically described by the mother of the philosopher Schopenhauer *(see the quote in the preface of this book).*

Jacobsen (1999) names three groups of behavioral characteristics that distinguish the gifted from the average person: observing, thinking/combining and reacting/acting.[8]

---

8   Jacobsen calls these, more basically: intensity, complexity and drive.

In our opinion these areas are linked to the physiological bases of high intelligence (see the preface). Depending on their attitude towards life, their social strategy, and developed skills, the three areas may evolve into 'downward behavior' (the passive, 'victimized' form), exaggerated behavior (the aggressive form), or a balanced behavior. As the introduction also describes, a gifted person, when in balance shows the following characteristics:

- highly intelligent (thinking)
- autonomous (being)
- multi-facetted emotional life (feeling)
- passionate and curious (wanting)
- highly sensitive (perceiving)
- creation-directed (doing)
- sparkling, original, quick, intense and complex (interplay)

We find many of these characteristics in many of our descriptions. A brief overview: Liz (chapter 1) quickly sizes up situations and is creative in finding new solutions. Jacob (chapter 2) has a gift for analyzing and delivering perfect work. Vincent (chapter 4) understands things quickly, and is strongly motivated to keep up with new developments in his field. We see the same with Edward (chapter 6).
Frances (chapter 7) is very involved in her work and is creative. She invents a new registration system almost as an afterthought.
Samantha (chapter 3) can also analyze very resolutely. Frances and Samantha are both very sensitive to stimuli. Malcolm (chapter 11) and Boris (chapter 10) have very broad interests and devote themselves to their jobs in a very driven way (whether asked or not). They also work on very diverse activities in and outside of their jobs.

Rose (chapter 9) has a very deep sense of justice.
Bastian (chapter 8) is averse to authority. Kitty (chapter 5) and Bastian (chapter 8) are very entrepreneurial and have lots of grit. They follow their own course.

Gifted people at their best are original, creative, critical, driven and productive employees. They are very valuable in their work and in society. But when they lose their balance, they fall into traps that can sometimes lead to destructive behavior. For example, we saw that Edward (chapter 6) showed such aggressive behavior that it frightened his colleagues. We also saw this excessive behavior in Bastian (chapter 8). In the view of their environment, they are no longer 'on track.' In Samantha's case (chapter 3), we saw the victim behavior version. Nobody understood her, she thought. Samantha went too far in her irritation and anger and started accusing everyone. Kitty (chapter 5) adapted to a high degree to what others wanted from her.

Gifted off course: unguided missiles?

A powerful personality who causes problems and does not have a clear profile and direction, conjures up the image of an unguided missile in his or her environment - someone who cannot be guided, who cannot cooperate with others, cannot be communicated with, a 'know it all', unsociable towards colleagues and supervisors (and also towards partners and friends).

Such behavior by the gifted not only creates irritation, but also fear and uncertainty. Some supervisors feel threatened, as happened in the cases of Liz (chapter 1), Edward (chapter 6) and Samantha (chapter 3). Such behavior often makes communicating more difficult. All of a sudden, both parties are entrenched in their positions and conflicts arise. The preceding chapters contain a great deal of information about this. We think that going off course has two sides and reflects the interplay between the gifted and his or her environment.

The gifted may quickly understand how things are put together; they can adapt quickly, enjoy a lot of things, and look for new solutions to problems. They are able to see new opportunities because of their deductive powers and do not really fit into a structured environment. These factors may create many problems not only in their work environment, but also in personal relationships.

Some employers like creative, enthusiastic employees. A gifted person can be a major source of inspiration within his or her environment. Other employers prefer adjusted, methodical employees, leaving little room for the gifted to be 'different.' The options for the gifted person who wants to keep his or her job are to wither away, or to adjust, potentially creating a loss of passion and enthusiasm. This may cause the individual to become increasingly irritated, quarreling about other people's mistakes; the pattern may lead to justifying themselves everywhere or to begin accusing others. The same passion that was once a strength becomes a trap.

The result is that such individuals no longer know what they do well; they lose contact with their feelings, no longer know what they want, and lose their inspiration. In short, they go off course.

In the cases we described, the most consistent problem is a breakdown in communication between the individual and his or her environment. Both sides start 'misunderstanding' each other. The environment often describes this situation in terms of 'being off course', as in the example of Jacob (chapter 2). Although it seems that we are dealing with an interaction between the gifted and their job environment, we chose (for this book) to start with the gifted individuals themselves. They have both the talent and the responsibility to influence their environment, although we know that there are limits to their ability to do so.

How does this process work exactly?
Although we think that a separate book can be written on this subject alone, we do have some observations regarding this, based on our cases.

'Falling back' on the brain

When they lose their balance, you often see gifted people 'falling back' on their talent: their intelligence. A gifted person tends to focus more on the content than on the process. Their focus on the content strengthens the feeling of not being recognized for what they are, i.e. different from other people, and that they are not valued for what drives them. The fear of not being recognized or valued, or even more strongly, feeling rejected, may result in a gifted person closing off his or her emotions or expressing them in a destructive way.

Obstructive thoughts also play a role, such as:

> I must be perfect,
> I am not allowed to make mistakes,
> Everybody must like me.

These are obstructive thoughts that occur very often, especially in gifted people. Most of our case profiles reveal this thought pattern.

We observed that when these gifted individuals went 'off course', they became very angry and blamed other people: Edward, (chapter 6), Bastian (chapter 8), Samantha (chapter 3), and Rose (chapter 9). Or they became depressed: Jacob (chapter 2); or had panic attacks: Boris (chapter 10). Sometimes they developed other physical problems: Vincent (chapter 4), Frances (chapter 7). In almost all cases, there were high degrees of rationalization. However, in the case of Liz (chapter 1), we saw the opposite – she was overwhelmed by her emotions.

In every case, to one degree or another, we found that these individuals lost contact with their own power and inspiration, resulting in losing the connection with their own environment.

Dealing with emotions

In nearly every case in this book we discuss individuals experiencing great difficulties in feeling their own emotions (including positive emotions). We believe that reconnecting with your feelings is the first step to get back on course. Experiencing no emotions or feeling only negative emotions also removes an individual's source of inspiration and drive. These subjects no longer know what they want for themselves, as we saw in the case of Vincent (chapter 4) and Kitty (chapter 5). For that reason we always pay a lot of attention to feelings while working with the gifted person.

No 'connection'

In many of these cases, we see that our subjects lose the 'connection' to their environment, resulting in part from their extremely quick observations and their critical thinking. What strikes us is that many gifted people communicate mainly at the objective content level and not on the emotional relationship level. Vincent (chapter 4) is a clear example of that. This 'one-sided' form of communicating does not encourage 'connecting' to the environment, least of all when the emotions have a 'negative' charge.

In addition, we also observe a number of obstructive factors during communication:

- Not daring to say what you want and can do: Frances (chapter 7), Kitty (chapter 5);
- Not listening to the other person: Boris (chapter 10);
- Blaming others: Rose (chapter 9);
- Arrogance, being pedantic: Jacob (chapter 2), Edward (chapter 6).

If, as a gifted person, you become aware that you no longer are connecting and you then train yourself to develop communication skills, you have taken a second step towards setting a new course. Vincent (chapter 4) and Edward (chapter 6) start to change the moment they realized this.

Hitting the target!

As we said before, when laying out these cases, we pay a lot of attention to these two aspects: dealing with emotions (feeling again) and relationships in the form of communication. We believe that these are the two most important elements for getting back on course. Our motive in writing this book was to provide guidance in how to do that.

We use a number of methods, including painting, drawing, hiking, writing stories, provocative coaching, and exploring core qualities. This is not an exhaustive list, but explains some of our ideas for connecting with gifted people, to provide support in their journey to regain balance in their lives. Of course as a gifted person you yourself play a large role in all of this.

Own responsibility

In the examples we described, many of the gifted people realize their own role in the situation only after problems (such as exhaustion or being fired) occur. They then become aware of:

- their talents and their effects on their environment;
- their motivation and passion;
- their specific traps which are closely connected to being gifted;
- other ways to deal with their talents and passions;
- other ways to explain their talents to their environment;
- a work environment that can do justice to their talents. The gifted need a work environment with the freedom to 'explore' and where they can unleash their creativity. These are important conditions for making their gifts visible.

For many of these individuals, this consciousness-raising becomes a sometimes difficult investigative process. What is happening here? What am I doing? Why do I react this way? Who am I? What do I really want? What drives me in my work and in my life? What is really important to me?
But the process also forces them to understand that

changing their interactions with their environment is a very important step in order to make effective changes. Are you willing to look at yourself? What is your part in the problems or conflicts that come up? If you focus only on whatever may be wrong with your boss, or your colleagues, or your organization, you are destined to fail.

Every change must begin with you. So, you have to choose to change. Starting your own investigation demands courage and guts, because there is no guidebook. General, well-meaning suggestions that may be useful for many people, do not automatically apply to the gifted.

Four basic questions for yourself
In summary, here are four basic questions you can ask yourself to find your course again:

- How do I reconnect with my own feelings and recognize what really moves me?
- Which obstructive thoughts do I have regarding myself and my environment?
- How do I recognize my inspiration and drive, and how do I regain those if I fall back into my negative patterns?
- How do I regain the connection with my environment?

By searching for answers to these questions most of the people we describe succeeded, with or without professional guidance, to escape their traps and return to a healthier course.

Changing with or without professional guidance?
In this book the search process for these gifted individuals occurs during interactions with a professional counselor. Of course, this is not always necessary. For example, Samantha (chapter 3) and Kitty (chapter 5) also talk with their girlfriends. A supervisor can also play a role

here, as happens in the cases of Malcolm (chapter 11) and Vincent (chapter 4). A frank conversation about how you function might be a good start.

Afterwards you can have a number of conversations with your personnel advisor, your Work and Organizational psychologist or your occupational physician, whatever you prefer. Sometimes a personal coach, who confronts you with a mirror and thinks along with you, may be useful. Support in the form of therapy might be worthwhile if many things bother you, or if you want to understand more about how things got this far.

If you don't feel well for whatever reason, for example, if you are depressed, it makes sense to contact your personal physician. Anti-depressants might sometimes lift you up out of a difficult time, so conversations with a coach or a psychologist make more sense.

If you think that you may have a personality disorder, call on a psychiatrist or a psychotherapist. You probably need long-term assistance by a professional in this field.

Finally

We wrote this book for the benefit of gifted people in their work environment. It is intended to be helpful to those who are insufficiently aware, or not at all aware, of their talents and what can happen in interactions with their environment. We hope this book will also prove to be helpful to those who want to make better use of their talents and want to create or co-create a working environment in which they can flourish and follow their passions. Last-but-not-least we hope this book will be a practical resource and inspiration for all professionals working with gifted people.

Information

This chapter contains brief background information on topics that are discussed in the book.

ADHD

ADHD is the abbreviation of 'Attention-Deficit/Hyperactivity Disorder.' It expresses itself in the form of restlessness, impulsive actions and problems with concentration. The symptoms of ADHD may look like (and may overlap with) those of giftedness but both can also occur at the same time. It is important to distinguish between both disorders because people suffering from ADHD can only be treated with medication combined with coaching and therapy.

More information about ADHD can be found at: http://www.mayoclinic.com/health/adult-adhd/DS01161
A self-test can be found at: http://www.mayoclinic.com/health/adult-adhd/DS01161
We recommend leaving diagnosis of ADHD to an expert in this field. Unfortunately, there are very few experts who work in both fields (ADHD and high-giftedness).

Autism

Autism is a developmental disorder with a strong genetic component. The proper term these days is Autism Spectrum Disorder (ASD). This set of disorders includes classic autism, Asperger's syndrome (no delays in cognitive development and language) and pervasive developmental disorder, not otherwise specified (commonly abbreviated as PDD-NOS). The latter diagnosis is given when the full set of criteria for autism or Asperger's syndrome are not met.

Asperger's syndrome occurs in people with either normal intelligence or high giftedness. The disorder occurs much more often in boys than in girls. Some people with Asperger's have an extraordinary memory for certain kinds of knowledge. (People with Asperger's are sometimes called 'idiot savants'). They often manage to mask their condition by using their high intelligence.
There is no cure for the condition. But a patient's functioning may improve by using structured programs. This may be done even later in life. Gifted people sometimes appear to suffer from Autism Spectrum Disorder because of their communication challenges (see this book). It is important to first determine whether this is the case in order to determine the appropriate guidance and coaching.
We recommend ASD only be diagnosed by an expert in this field. Unfortunately, there are very few experts who work in both fields (ASD and giftedness).

CANS

CANS is the abbreviation for Complaints of Arm, Neck and/or Shoulder.
The CANS model provides a template for all complaints of the arms, hands, neck or shoulders not linked to an acute wound (such as broken bones) or a general illness (like rheumatism). CANS covers complaints like pain, stiffness, tingling or loss of power (shown for example by writing more sloppily than before).
Until recently, the term RSI (Repetitive Strain Injury) was used to describe these problems. This term is less correct because there is no injury and there is almost never a repetitive strain. In almost every case there are repeated movements and long-term static stresses.

CANS often involves a combination of the following factors.

- *Physical stress*
  By often making the same movement, a group of muscles or a tendon may become irritated.

Continuous pressure or maintaining an unnatural posture might lead to overstressing muscles. Vibration may also lead to complaints.

- *Mental pressure*
  Working under tight deadlines, experiencing high intellectual demands during work or experiencing a high pressure for other job-related reasons may lead to a higher level of muscle tension when combined with a poor workplace arrangement or a negative work environment. Such circumstances may contribute to a long-lasting problem.

- *Personal factors*
  Being a 'perfectionist' (not allowing yourself to make mistakes) may also contribute to CANS. An individual's ability to tolerate physical and emotional stress likely plays a role as well.

In fact, perfectionism may be one of the most important reasons that gifted people often suffer from CANS. The proper approach in those cases is making these individuals more aware of the way they perform their jobs and teaching them how to relax regularly.

Depression

In order to diagnose depression, several of the following conditions must be present.

The two most important symptoms of depression are:
- feeling depressed, feeling 'empty'
- loss of interest and joy, no longer being able to experience pleasure

In order to diagnose depression several of the following seven complaints or symptoms must also be present for an extended time:
- a feeling of worthlessness or guilt
- sleeping disorders

- decrease or increase in appetite or marked changes in weight
- little energy or feeling tired
- problems with concentrating or making decisions
- sluggishness or a continuous feeling of agitation
- Recurring thoughts about death or suicide.

Reliable medical information about major depression can be found here:
http://www.mayoclinic.com/health/depression/DS00175.

Individuals will find many self-tests on the Internet that can be used as a first step in finding out whether they suffer from depression. If there are indications that you are, we advise you to contact a physician and/or a psychologist immediately. There is a range of treatment options.

High sensitivity
Giftedness often goes together with high sensitivity which can express itself in various areas: psychomotoric, sensual, intellectual, imaginative, emotional aspects and may look like ADHD. Many gifted people suffer from high sensitivity.

Sensory over-stimulation may reveal itself aurally (noisy equipment, radios, sounds made during eating), visually (light) or in a tactile way (certain materials, labels in clothing or touching). Sensitivity for sound and other auditory stimuli (e.g. a shopping mall full of people) often occurs in the gifted. Therefore we provide some additional information.

Sensitivity to sound
Someone who is highly sensitive to sounds has trouble concentrating in very noisy environments. The government sets standards for sound levels in work areas. Those standards depend on the nature of the work.
In the Netherlands, no more than 80 dB(A) is allowed during a full workday.

This level can cause damage, not just discomfort and is approximately equivalent to the noise level measured alongside a highway. A normal conversation has a level of 60 dB(A), a vacuum cleaner 70 dB(A).

Highly sensitive people probably have much lower thresholds for sound. It may be compared with suffering from an allergy. The real question is: what can and must an employer do to respond? In principle, exposure should be as low as possible. For example, people with an allergy to certain animals and who work in animal testing may be able to use personal protective equipment and/or medication to alleviate the symptoms. However, this is not possible in cases of oversensitivity to sound. Earplugs might be a possibility, but they make working more difficult.

An employer may not be able to provide a highly sensitive worker with a separate workspace, nor assure that other employees/colleagues will accept such an accommodation. Good employer practices require the employer to explore options together with the employee. However, this may cause the employee to realize that there is no perfect solution.

Overstrain and burnout

Overstrain may result from too much stress or too many demands (demands from outside and self-imposed demands) on the one hand and too few opportunities to alleviate the stress on the other. A procedure based on a set of weighing scales model often helps clarify the process. The balance between a 'burden' and the 'ability to carry the burden' is upset. Complaints related to stress may be considered a signal to slow down, or to decrease the stress. However, if that is impossible for the individual and the person remains exposed to serious stress, the end result is often nervousness. In this case the individual may feel he/she is losing his/her grip on the situation. Often, something happens to trigger the situation.

The complaints that accompany overstrain are:

- psychological tension, such as worrying, being stressed, irritable, having problems sleeping, depression and crying easily
- symptoms of physical and mental exhaustion such as being tired, listless, having problems thinking and concentrating, lack of drive and no longer being interested in anything
- the feeling of 'not being able to cope'

In addition there are often physical tensions such as headaches, dizziness, chest pains, heart palpitations or stomach complaints.
We speak of 'overstrain' when the complaints are so severe that an individual is no longer able to function normally, e.g. doing his or her job.
Every year 5-10% of adults suffer from overstrain at least once.

We often see a combination of circumstances causing overstrain:

- obligations: work, household, personal activities
- life events: illness (also of a loved one), moving, having a child, divorce, death
- problems: with yourself, with others (at work or elsewhere), housing, and finances.

Half of the people with overstrain are fully back at work after six weeks and three-quarters of them return to work within three months. Almost everybody is cured after six months. Active intervention makes all the difference.

In a very few cases these problems remain so severe that the person needs to apply for disability payments or lose his/her job.
Going back to work is more important than solving the complaints. After all: by returning to work (however, gradually and with professional help), most people often recover.

In the past overstrain often led to long breaks from work and receiving disability payments. Recovering from overstrain typically occurs in three phases, which blend into each other.

1. *The crisis phase:* the individual processes and accepts his/her overstrain and begins to understand it. Rest and relaxation to surmount the most serious balance disorders. This phase usually takes a few days to a few weeks.
2. *The problem and solution phase:* the individual identifies the problems that caused the exhaustion and considers possible solutions.
3. *The implementation phase:* the individual implements the solutions and gradually resumes his/her work.

'Burn out' can be considered a serious form of overstrain. On average we believe burn out takes two years to develop and is almost always related to work issues. The diagnosis is based on three groups of symptoms:

1. *Emotional and physical exhaustion.* Feelings of extreme tiredness and being dejected. A combination of physical and psychological complaints. Crying fits also occur frequently.
2. *Depersonalization.* Less interest in one's environment, becoming cynical and losing interest in others. Derealization: feeling as if you are 'outside of your own body'.
3. *Feeling of increasing incompetence.* Thinking one can no longer meet expectations. This may result in a vicious circle, leading a patient to start working even harder.

Literature, informative websites and high IQ organizations

Literature alphabetical

Attwood, T. The Complete Guide to Asperger's Syndrome. Jessica Kingsley, London/ Philadelphia, 2007.

Burger-Veltmeijer, A. E. J. Gifted or autistic? The 'grey zone'. In: K. Tirri & M. Ubani (Eds), Policies and programs in gifted education. Helsinki: University of Helsinki, 2007. (isbn: 978-952-10-3854-9)

Corten, F. G, Nauta, A. P., & Ronner, S. The highly intelligent and innovation. Key to innovation? Academic paper for the HRD conference in Amsterdam, October 2006. See websites www.werkenwaarde.nl, www.noksnauta.nl, www.meriones.nl

Deary, Ian J. Intelligence. A very short introduction. Oxford University Press, Oxford, 2001.

Ellis, A. & Harper, R. A. A new guide to rational living. Prentice-Hall, Upper Saddle River, New Jersey.1975.

Jackson, D. D., Beavin, J. H. & Watzlawick, P. Pragmatics of Human Communication. A study of Interactional Patterns, Pathologies and Paradoxes. W. W. Norton & Company, New York, NY, 1967.

Jacobsen, Mary-Elaine. The gifted Adult. Ballantine Books, New York, 1999.

Kooijman – van Thiel, M. B. G. M. (ed). Hoogbegaafd, dat zie je zo! Over zelfbeeld en imago van hoogbegaafden (Gifted, obvious! On identity and self-image of Gifted Persons). (Only available in Dutch.) Ede: OYA Productions, 2008.

Nauta, Noks, & Corten, Frans. Hoogbegaafden aan het werk. (Gifted adults at work.) Tijdschrift voor Bedrijfs- en Verzekeringsgeneeskunde (Journal for Occupational and Insurance Medicine) (TBV) 2002; 10(11): 332-335. See websites www.noksnauta.nl, www.werkenwaarde.nl.

Ofman, Daniel D. Core Qualities - A gateway to human resources. Spectrum, Schiedam, 2001.

Stewart, I & Joines, V. TA Today. A New Introduction to Transactional Analysis. Lifespace publishing, Chapel Hill, NC, 2012. (This is a new version of their 1987 book).

Streznewski, Marylou Kelly. Gifted Grownups. John Wiley & Sons, Inc., New York, Chichester, Weinheim, Brisbane, Singapore, Toronto, 1999.

Webb, J.T., Amend, E.R., Webb, N.E., Goerss, J., Beljan, P. & Olenchak, F.R. Misdiagnosis and dual diagnoses of gifted children and adults. Great Potential Press, Inc., Scottsdale, Arizona, 2005.

Yalom, I.D. The Schopenhauer cure. HarperCollins, New York, 2005.

Informative websites
Assessments for disability pensions in the Netherlands
http://www.biomedcentral.com/1471-2458/11/1

CANS (complaints of arm, neck and shoulder) article from 2007
http://www.biomedcentral.com/1471-2474/8/68

Headache, medical information
http://www.mayoclinic.com/health/chronic-daily-head-aches/DS00646

IQ-test online
http://www.iq-test.com/

Locus of Control
http://www.iq-tester.nl/locusofcontrol.htm
http://www.vanderbilt.edu/nursing/kwallston/mhlcscales.htm
http://www.med.usf.edu/~kmbrown/Locus_of_Control_
Overview.htm

Pain, chronic pain
http://www.nlm.nih.gov/medlineplus/pain.html

High IQ organizations

For some gifted people joining a High IQ organization can mean a lot. Here they can meet other people who are gifted, and often feel more accepted and at ease than ever before in their lives. However, some gifted people do not feel the need to meet other (gifted) people in person. Many of the contacts in these societies are virtual contacts, through email lists and discussion forums.

Here are some of the largest international high IQ organizations.

Mensa
www.mensa.org
Mensa is the oldest, largest, and the most well known High IQ organization. It was founded in Oxford in 1946 by Lancelot Ware, a lawyer and scientist, and Roland Berill, also an attorney. They wanted to form an organization that was non-political and open to all, regardless of race, origin and religion. Mensa's three goals are: to provide a stimulating intellectual and social environment for its members, to identify and foster human intelligence for the benefit of humanity, and to encourage research into the nature, characteristics, and uses of intelligence.

Mensa accepts members who score in the 98 percentile or higher on standardized and supervised tests.
Recognized tests are organized by Mensa itself, or a prospective member can submit a test score provided by a

licensed psychologist (not in all countries). Mensa doesn't issue opinions unless they are associated with the work of the association, but members are, of course, free to publish their own. Worldwide Mensa has approximately 110,000 members. The majority of the members are in the U.S. (American Mensa), the United Kingdom (British Mensa) and in Germany.

Intertel
www.intertel-iq.org
Intertel is the second oldest High IQ organization (after Mensa). It was founded in 1966 by Ralph Haines and was initially called International Legion of Intelligence. Its members are called 'Illians' and they are mainly from the U.S., with some members in Europe (mostly in the U.K. and Germany). Members communicate mainly through a 'Top1' mailing list but the organization also holds Annual Gatherings and some regional and private meetings (often together with Mensa). The goal of Intertel is similar to Mensa. The organization's motto is 'Participation and Excellence'.

International Society for Philosophical Enquiry (ISPE)
www.thethousand.com
ISPE is the first society created for people who are at the 0.1% percentile level of intelligence or above. It was founded as 'The Thousand' in 1974 by Dr Christopher Harding. Its goal is to become a modern equivalent of the ancient institutes for advanced studies and research, with some of the features of the seventeenth and eighteenth century scientific and philosophical societies. Today ISPE has about 600 members in 33 countries and territories. It accepts not only standardized tests but also a self-administered test designed by one of its members. The Society is unique among high IQ organizations with its hierarchical structure. Once a candidate is accepted he/she becomes an 'associate member', without the right to vote or hold office. Promotion to regular membership is based on achievements within the society and outside. It has a quarterly magazine called *Telicom*.

Triple Nine Society
www.triplenine.org
Another organization for people with a 1 in 1000 intelligence is the Triple Nine Society. It was created in 1978 and – as 'A Short (and Bloody) History of the High I.Q. Societies'[9] states – it is 'a more democratic alternative to ISPE'. It has five 'Founding Fathers' : Richard Canty, Ronald Hoeflin, Ronald Penner, Edgar Van Vleck, and Kevin Langdon - the latter is the most active founder. It accepts all applicants who score at or above the 99.9 percentile on specified supervised IQ tests (like Mensa and Intertel it does not accept unsupervised or online tests). The Triple Nine society's monthly publication is called *Vidya*. Members of this organization hold annual meetings (ggg999 in the U.S. and egg999 in Europe) which are open to members of other 99.9% organizations which have credible admission criteria (e.g. ISPE, One In A thousand society etc.).

High IQ Society
http://www.highiqsociety.org
The International High IQ Society represents a contemporary movement to encourage discussions on a variety of intellectual topics. It provides its members with a platform to present their ideas, discuss them in a friendly environment, and make learning enjoyable. Membership is open to people with an IQ score in the top five percent of the population.

---

9   See web page at http://www.eskimo.com/~miyaguch/history.html

Authors

Noks Nauta (1947) studied medicine and then worked as a school physician, an occupational physician, and as a specialist in occupational infectious diseases. She also taught occupational physicians, was a coordinator of education for primary care physicians, and a scientist at the Centre of Excellence of The Netherlands Society for Occupational Medicine. In 1999 she also graduated with a degree in Work and Organizational Psychology.

She is interested in how health care employees work and how they interact with each other, and she is especially active in the field of interprofessional cooperation and ethical deliberation. Within this area she also carries out research and provides training. She received her PhD in 2004 with the thesis: 'A matter of trust? About cooperation between primary care doctors and occupational physicians.'

Since 2000 she has worked in the field of gifted adults, especially with regards to their relationship with their work. She supports the gifted themselves by providing them with information about this subject, and also provides information to professionals (like psychologists and physicians) and Human Resource Management experts. She has written a number of articles about this subject and teaches workshops.

In 2010 she founded the Institute for Gifted and Talented Adults (www.ihbv.nl).
In 2012, she co-wrote, with Janneke Breedijk, a book for and about gifted teenagers.
In 2010 she co-wrote a book with her son Jelle Kok: 'The Innovation Brewery, From idea to innovation' (Pearson Publishers).
Her website is www.noksnauta.nl

Sieuwke Ronner (1951) studied clinical psychology graduating with a degree in health psychology. Later she also added a degree in Work and Organizational Psychology. Since 2002 she has been an independent advisor on work and health issues, a coach, a trainer and a mediator. She has experience both in the for-profit sector (business services, public housing organizations) and the non-profit sector (government, education, health care).

Her specialty is assisting in processes for change and providing training for associated courses; she provides training and personal coaching, focusing on vision development, cooperation, conflict management and negotiation. In addition, she counsels people during times of (imminent) health-related absenteeism from work.

Her approach is characterized by providing both a balanced distance from and involvement with the client, combined with a sharp eye for the uniqueness and vulnerability of individual employees.

Since 2002, through her work with Noks Nauta, she has become involved in guiding gifted people in their jobs. Through her experience in various organizations and with a number of gifted people in her immediate environment, she can easily connect with the way gifted people experience their lives.

Together with Noks Nauta, she teaches workshops for the gifted (including training in dealing with work-related stress). Her website is www.meriones.nl

17776196R00094

Printed in Great Britain
by Amazon